Beginning
Spanish
for the Utterly
CONFUSED

Beginning Spanish

for the

Utterly CONFUSED

Second Edition

Jean Yates, Ph.D.

New York Chicago San Francisco Lisbon London Madrid Mexico City
Milan New Delhi San Juan Seoul Singapore Sydney Toronto

Copyright © 2010 by The McGraw-Hill Companies, Inc. All rights reserved. Printed in the
United States of America. Except as permitted under the United States Copyright Act of
1976, no part of this publication may be reproduced or distributed in any form or by any
means, or stored in a database or retrieval system, without the prior written permission of
the publisher.

    3 4 5 6 7 8 9 10 11 12 13 14 15   QFR/QFR   1 9 8 7 6 5 4 3

ISBN 978-0-07-173963-4 (book and CD set)
MHID   0-07-173963-7 (book and CD set)

ISBN 978-0-07-173961-0 (book for set)
MHID   0-07-173961-0 (book for set)

Library of Congress Control Number: 2009942868

Trademarks: McGraw-Hill, the McGraw-Hill Publishing logo, Utterly Confused, and related
trade dress are trademarks or registered trademarks of The McGraw-Hill Companies
and/or its affiliates in the United States and other countries and may not be used without
written permission. All other trademarks are the property of their respective owners. The
McGraw-Hill Companies is not associated with any product or vendor mentioned in this
book.

McGraw-Hill books are available at special quantity discounts to use as premiums and
sales promotions or for use in corporate training programs. To contact a representative,
please e-mail us at bulksales@mcgraw-hill.com.

Enhanced CD

The accompanying disk (at the back of the book) contains audio recordings that can be
played on a standard CD player. These recordings are also included in MP3 format,
incorporating text that accompanies the audio. For the iPod or similar MP3 player:

1. Insert the disk into your computer.
2. Open the disk via My Computer.
3. Drag the folder "Beginning_Spanish_MP3s" into the Music Library of iTunes.
4. Sync your iPod with iTunes, and then locate the files on your player under:
   ARTISTS › Spanish: Beginning Spanish for the Utterly Confused

This book is printed on acid-free paper.

Contents

Where in the World Is Spanish Spoken?

A   España

B   Los Estados Unidos
C   México
D   Guatemala
E   El Salvador
F   Honduras
G   Nicaragua
H   Costa Rica
I   Panamá
J   Cuba
K   La República Dominicana
L   Puerto Rico

M   Venezuela
N   Colombia
O   Ecuador
P   Perú
Q   Bolivia
R   Chile
S   Argentina
T   Uruguay
U   Paraguay
V   Guinea Ecuatorial

Islas Baleares

Islas Canarias

A Special Message to the Utterly Confused Spanish Student

Spanish is the native language of the people of Spain and of nineteen countries in the Americas and in one small country in Africa, Equatorial Guinea. It is also widely spoken in the United States, both as a first and a second language. Still, it is not unusual to hear students say they are disappointed that they cannot speak Spanish well, even after years of study; that they don't understand Spanish grammar; that they are, indeed, confused.

Why Is Spanish Confusing?

Spanish Sounds Are Different from English Sounds

and they are put together according to a different pattern. At first, it doesn't seem possible that we could ever understand the series of staccato sounds of Spanish speakers. It seems that they speak much faster than we do.

> **Solution:** Learn how each sound is made, then how it relates to other sounds, then practice making the sounds. Read aloud, say your dialogues aloud, and keep practicing. Remember that pronunciation is a skill that has to be practiced to be learned. Don't worry if your pronunciation sounds funny to you at first—it should sound very different from English.

Each Region Has Its Own Way of Speaking

Argentines, Mexicans, Spaniards, and Peruvians all have different accents, just as do Alabamans, New Yorkers, Londoners, and Australians. When people from different regions get together, they often compare the way they speak: You say it this way; we say it that way. However, they are able to understand each other when they avoid the words and expressions that are used only in their own regions.

Solution: When we learn Spanish as a second language, we learn the *standard* variety—one that can be understood in all Spanish-speaking areas.

Spanish Words Are Put Together According to a System That Is Very Different from the English System

Spanish not only uses different words, but also sometimes different verb tenses and different word order than English does to convey the same meaning. We cannot, therefore, translate English word-for-word into Spanish—the result would be unintelligible.

Solution: Learn phrases, units, and patterns rather than single words. Always practice meaningful expressions in context, and you will automatically use them correctly. You will begin to think in Spanish rather than translate from English.

Spanish and English Often Get Their Signals Crossed

It often happens that a Spanish word, expression, verb tense, or other grammatical element has an exact equivalent in English—for some purposes. However, for other purposes, this same element doesn't work.

Solution: Learn the meanings and messages of words, phrases, and grammatical elements in the contexts in which they are used.

There Is Too Much to Learn. How Will I Ever Learn to Say Everything I Want to Say?

Solution: Start learning and speaking right away. Be patient, but be determined. Keep practicing. When you reach a plateau, read aloud in Spanish. It works. Remember, Rome wasn't built in a day, but it was built!

How to Study Spanish

Does the word *grammar* scare you away from Spanish classes? If so, you are not alone. Following are the two most common statements heard by students beginning their study of Spanish.

- "How can I learn Spanish grammar when I don't even understand English grammar?"
- "I don't want to learn grammar, I just want to learn to speak the language so I can talk to my friends (or people I work with, or people I'll meet when I travel.)"

The answers to these questions should encourage you. First, if you speak English, then you know English grammar. To prove it, take the following grammar test.

Read the following sentence, then answer the questions. Some of the words are imaginary—this is done on purpose to illustrate how much meaning *grammar* conveys, even when we don't know the meaning of some words.

A gib sorbed up the zork and finted his bont.

1. Is this sentence about the past, the present, or the future?
2. If the same thing happens tomorrow, what will happen?
3. If the same thing happens every day, how would you say that?
4. How many "actors" are there in this sentence?
5. What would you call the "actor" you identified in question 4? What would you call two of them?
6. Is the gib an animal or an inanimate object?
7. Is the gib male or female?

8. What does the gib have? What would you call two of them?

9. How many things did the gib do?

10. Which one did he do first?

11. Describe the gib with a real or imaginary word and put the word where it belongs in the sentence.

12. Describe the gib's first action with a real or imaginary word and put the word where it belongs in the sentence.

Check your answers at the end of this chapter.

Let's analyze our example sentence. First of all, it consists of two kinds of words, content words and function words. The content words are the ones that have been made up. The function words are the ones you are already familiar with. Look at the following chart.

Content Words	Function Words
gib	a
sorb	up
zork	the
fint	and
bont	his

Just looking at the words in the chart does not enable you to answer the questions on the test. What enabled you to answer the questions is your knowledge of English grammar.

Here are some of the *rules* you used.

1. The word *a* indicates a singular noun. (gib)

2. A noun is made plural by adding -*s*. (gibs)

3. The order of a sentence is: actor + action. (A gib sorbed)

4. *and* joins two like elements. (sorbed and finted)

5. -*ed* indicates past action. (sorbed, finted)

6. *and* separates and orders two past actions chronologically.

7. *his* indicates possession by a male person or other animal.

8. *big*—or the descriptive word you used—goes before the word it describes. (big gib)

9. *slowly*—or the word you used—can go either before or after the action word. (slowly sorbed / sorbed slowly)

So What's the Point of All This?

The point is that grammar is important because language *is* grammar, and the grammar of each language is unique. Grammar is the set of patterns that all speakers of a language use to communicate with each other. We can learn those patterns—and produce an unlimited number of meaningful sentences—or we could sit down and memorize, say, five hundred "useful phrases." Which is more efficient?

Don't Forget

Grammar *rules* are not arbitrary laws that we are told to obey; rather, they are like the *rules* on a piece of wide-ruled or college-ruled paper: patterns that guide us in the right direction.

Now let's set up a plan to learn the same kind of information about Spanish. First, we will separate vocabulary into two categories: (1) *content words* and (2) *function words or phrases*.

Content Words

We will learn how each type of content word can be used or changed or substituted for, enabling us to talk about what we want to talk about. Once you have learned how each type of content word works in a sentence, you will be given the green light to use a Spanish-English dictionary to look up new words that are in the same category. In the Appendix at the back of this book are pages designed to help you get started with a personal vocabulary list (**Vocabulario personal**) of content words, and as you follow the lessons in the book, you will receive guidelines for carrying out this ongoing project. The **Vocabulario personal** list of content words is divided into four categories:

     A. **Sustantivos:** Nouns (words like *gib* and *zork* and *bont*)
     B. **Adjetivos:** Adjectives (words like *big* or the one you made up for that slot)
     C. **Verbos:** Verbs (words like *sorb* and *fint*)
     D. **Adverbios:** Adverbs (words like *slowly* or the one you made up for that slot)

Function Words

We will also learn how function words and phrases are used to form the framework for the content words, considering the patterns of Spanish, rather than trying to put Spanish words together according to English patterns.

The function words and phrases will be introduced in the context of dialogues—examples of typical conversations—that you will be asked to memorize. This activity may seem unnecessary or boring, because the conversation may have nothing to do with your personal life; however, in memorizing the dialogues, you are practicing the framework of Spanish, learning to use function words correctly and in the proper order, and most importantly, *not translating from English.* As soon as you have memorized each dialogue, you will be able to substitute your own personal content words for the ones given, and you will be producing your own sentences—correctly, without thinking about *rules.*

It is important to keep in mind that people have, or are capable of, similar thoughts, feelings, and reactions, regardless of their native language. It is just as important to realize that each language uses a different system to organize this information. In order to learn Spanish, then, we must learn its *system:* its regular patterns and the exceptions to those patterns.

Answers to the Test

1. the past   2. A gib will sorb up the zork and fint his bont.   3. A gib sorbs up the zork and fints his bont.   4. one   5. a gib, gibs   6. an animal   7. male   8. a bont, bonts 9. two   10. He sorbed up the zork.   11. *big/?*, between *A* and *gib*   12. *slowly/?*, before or after *sorbed*

How to Pronounce Spanish

Look over this chapter quickly to get a general idea of Spanish pronunciation, then refer to it from time to time, practicing the individual sounds separately. Listen to the Pronunciation Section on the recording that accompanies this book, and follow the speakers' instructions as you look at the letters, words, and sentences on pages xvi–xxii of this book. Good pronunciation takes a lot of practice— but it is definitely worth the effort.

Do I Need to Read This Chapter?

➡ When I see a Spanish word written, do I know how to pronounce it?

➡ When I hear Spanish spoken, do I know how the sounds are spelled?

➡ Do I know how Spanish vowels and consonants differ in pronunciation from their counterparts in English?

➡ Do I understand the purpose of written accent marks?

How Is the Spanish Alphabet Different from the English Alphabet?

All of the letters in the English alphabet are also in the Spanish alphabet. Spanish has, in addition, the letters **ll, ñ,** and **rr.**

The Spanish alphabet, then, has five vowel letters:

a e i o u

and twenty-four consonant letters:

b c d f g h j k l ll m n ñ p q r rr s t v w x y z

Under special circumstances, accent marks may appear over vowel letters.

á é í ó ú

The letter **u** after the letter **g** may have a **diérisis: gü**

Are the Sounds for Each Spanish Letter the Same as English Sounds?

No. Spanish has a few sounds that are the same as English sounds, some that are similar, and some that do not occur in English. In addition, a sound that is represented by a letter in English can be represented by a different letter in Spanish. This can be quite confusing!

Look at the letters and try to pronounce them according to the Spanish patterns. You may want to mark problem letters—those that are different from English.

First, learn to pronounce the vowels. There are only five, and they are always pronounced the same—in every dialect of Spanish!

1. To make each vowel, first open your mouth to the beginning position for the suggested similar sound in English.

2. Make a sound and do not move your lips or jaw. If your mouth is in the right shape, the vowel sound will be correct.

   a is similar to the doctor's *ah* (don't move your jaw!).
   e is similar to the *e* in *effort.*
   i is similar to the *ee* in *week* (smile wide and freeze it).
   o is similar to the *o* in *Los* of *Los Angeles.*
   u is similar to the *u* in *tuba* (stop and freeze before rounding your lips).

3. Two vowels can occur together. If one of them is an **i** or a **u,** they are considered to be one unit. (Be sure to freeze your lips and jaw on the second sound.)

i before another vowel sounds like an English *y*.

ia *(ya)*   **ie** *(ye)*   **io** *(yo)*   **iu** *(yu)*

u before another vowel sounds like an English *w*.

ua *(wa)*   **ue** *(we)*   **ui** *(wi)*   **uo** *(wo)*

i or **u** after another vowel also fuses two sounds into one syllable. English words with similar sounds are given in parentheses.

ai *(eye)*   **ei** *(<u>eight</u>)*   **oi** *(b<u>oy</u>)*   **ui** *(<u>week</u>)*
au *(a oo)*   **eu** *(e oo)*   **iu** *(<u>you</u>)*

4. When a written accent mark occurs over one of these vowels, two syllables should be pronounced. Pronounce the vowel with the accent mark with more emphasis. (The English pronunciations given here are only approximations—keep your lips and jaw tight, as before.)

   ía *(ee' ah)*   **íe** *(ee' eh)*   **ío** *(ee' o)*

   úa *(oo' ah)*   **úe** *(oo' eh)*   **úi** *(oo' ee)*   **úo** *(oo' o)*

   aí *(ah ee')*   **eí** *(eh ee')*   **oí** *(o ee')*

   aú *(ah oo')*   **eú** *(eh oo')*

5. When the other vowels occur together, they glide from one sound to the other, forming two syllables.

   ae *(ah' eh)*   **ao** *(ah' o)*

   ea *(eh' ah)*   **ee** *(eh' eh)*   **eo** *(eh' o)*

   oa *(o' ah)*   **oe** *(o' eh)*   **oo** *(o' o)*

6. The letter **y** after a vowel is pronounced exactly like the Spanish vowel **i**.

   hay *(eye)*   **ley** *(lay)*   **hoy** *(oy)*   **muy** *(mwee)*

Now practice the vowel sounds as you learn the consonant sounds.

1. The letters **b** and **v** represent the same Spanish sound. It is similar to the *b* in *but*.

   base   bebe   bife   bobo   bus
   vaso   veo   vino   voz   vulgar

2. The letter **c** before the vowels **a, o,** or **u** is similar to the *k* in *walking*.

   café   coco   cuna

Before **e** or **i** this sound is spelled **qu.**

queso   química   tequila

The letter **k** occurs only in foreign words, like the words **kilo** and **kilogramo.**
cu before another vowel is pronounced like the *qu* in *quick.*

cuando   cueva   cuidado   cuota

3. The letter **c** before the vowels **e** or **i**, and the letter **z** before **a, o,** or **u,** are pronounced in Latin America like *s* as in *sun.* In much of Spain they are pronounced like the *th* of *thumb.*

zapato   cena   cinco   zorro   zumo

The letter **s** is also pronounced—in Latin America and in Spain—like *s* as in *sun.*

sala   se   si   solo   Susana

4. The letters **ch** together are just like the *ch* in *chip.*

cha-cha-chá   cheque   chico   choza   chulo

5. The letter **d** at the beginning of a word is similar to the *d* in *dinner.* Between vowels it is like the *th* in *brother.*

dama   dedo   diga   donde   duda

6. The letter **f** is pronounced like the *f* in *father.*

fama   feo   finca   fórmula   fuma

7. a. The letter **g** before **a, o,** or **u** at the beginning of a word is similar to the *g* in *girl.* Before the letters **e** or **i** this sound is spelled **gu.**

gana   gueto   guía   goce   gusto

Between vowels it has a sound that does not occur in English, but is like the French *r.* It's like *g* (as in *girl*) with a sore throat—let the air come through the passage instead of stopping it.

amiga   pague   águila   amigo   agudo

b. **gu** before **a** or **o** can be pronounced like *gw* or like the *w* in *wash.* This sound before **e** or **i** is spelled **gü.**

guantes   güera   güito   averiguo

The letter **w** is used only for foreign words.

c. **g** before **e** or **i** can be pronounced like a strong *h* as in *Help!* In many dialects it has a Scottish-like *ch* sound, as in *Loch,* or like the German *Ach!* It is like the **g** between vowels, as described in 7a, only with no voice sound.

gesto   general   gimnasio   gigante   gitano

The letter **j** has the same pronunciation.

jaleo   jefe   jirafa   joya   jugo

8. The letter **h** is always silent, just like the *h* in *honest.*

    hago   hecho   hijo   honesto   Hugo

9. The letter **l** at the beginning of a syllable is similar to *l* as in *lost.*

    lava   leche   liso   los   luna

    At the end of a syllable it is a bit like *t'll* as in "What'll we do?"

    al   del   albañil   alcohol   Raúl

10. **ll** is considered one letter. It can be pronounced like *yy* as in "Say yes!" or like *j* as in *jar.*

    llave   llevo   allí   llora   lluvia

    The letter **y** at the beginning of a syllable has the same two possible pronunciations.

    ya   yeso   yin   yo   yuca

11. The letter **m** is pronounced like the *m* in *man.*

    mamá   mes   mima   mono   música

12. The letter **n** is usually pronounced like the *n* in *name.*

    nada   necio   ni   no   nudo

    Before a syllable beginning with **ca, que, qui, co, cu,** or **ga, gue, gui, go, gu,** it is pronounced like the *ng* of *sing.*

    nunca   tanque   yanqui   banco   vínculo
    venga   merengue   anguila   mango   ángulo

13. The letter **ñ** is pronounced like the *ni* of *onion.*

    niña   niñera   compañía   año

14. The letter **p** is pronounced like the *p* of *spin.* It is not followed by a puff of air like the English *p* at the beginning of a word, making it sound close to an English *b.*

    pan   Pepe   piña   pobre   púa

15. The pronunciation of **r** is nothing like the English *r*. You may want to mark this letter at first to remind yourself of this. It is much more similar to the underlined letters in the following English words:

English word	Similar Spanish pronunciation (but keep your vowels frozen)
bo*d*y	bari
Be*tt*y	veri
Ey*d*ie	iri
ough*tt*a	hora

    r at the beginning of a word is pronounced exactly like **rr,** described in 16, below.

16. The combination **rr** has a trilled sound that can be learned with practice. To learn to make it:

    a. With the tip of your tongue, find a spot behind your top teeth.

    b. Open your mouth wide, bringing your tongue down.

    c. Bring your mouth to an almost closed position, keeping your lips open. As you do this, place your tongue loosely on the spot you found in 16a. The air that comes through as you close your mouth will cause the tongue to tap repeatedly. Make a sound with your voice as you do this.

jarra	torre	arriba	arroz	arruina
rana	recibo	río	rosa	ruinas

Don't Forget

You can learn to make this sound. Just keep practicing.

17. The letter **t** is similar to the *t* of *sting*. It is not followed by the puff of air that accompanies the *t* at the beginning of a word in English.

    taza   techo   tiza   toro   tuna

18. The letter **x** is like the sound of *ks* in *works*.

    exacto   excepto   exijo   léxico   exótico   exhumo

    x in the word **México**—and in some other words of Mexican origin—is pronounced like the **j** and **ge/gi** sounds (see 7c.)

What Are Accent Marks For?

An accent mark—called a **tilde** in Spanish—is used

- over the emphasized vowel in a question word:

¿Quién . . . ?	¿Dónde . . . ?	¿Por qué . . . ?	¿Cuándo . . . ?
Who?	*Where?*	*Why?*	*When?*

- over the vowel of certain one-syllable words that have homonyms with different meanings:

sí	si	él	el	tú	tu
yes	*if*	*he*	*the*	*you*	*your*
té	te	mí	mi	más	mas
tea	*you*	*me*	*my*	*more*	*but*

- over the emphasized vowel of a word that does *not* conform to the following patterns:

    1. A word that ends in a vowel, a one-syllable vowel combination, or an **n** or an **s** is emphasized on the next-to-last syllable:

Words that end in a vowel

amiga   leche   mini   lobo   guru
hamaca   completo   practico canoso   tumulto

Words that end in a one-syllable vowel combination

gloria   especie   estudio
agua   abue   contiguo

Words that end in -n

cocinan   leen   abren   examen

Words that end in -s

cocinas   lees   abres   cocinamos

Exceptions to the pattern require a **tilde**.

ácido   estudió   están   estación
exámenes   espérame   estímulo brújula

2. A word that ends in any consonant other than **n** or **s** is emphasized on the final syllable:

d   **j**   **l**   **r**   **y**   **z**
ciudad   reloj   animal   trabajar   estoy   arroz

Exceptions to the pattern require a **tilde**.

árbol   almíbar   lápiz
difícil   alcázar   González

Why Do I Have Trouble Hearing Individual Words in Spanish?

Spanish words are all run together; there is rarely a break between words. Also, when a word that begins with a vowel follows a word that ends with the same vowel, the vowel is only pronounced once. Practice this by reading aloud, linking the words as follows:

Jaime es mi amigo.   (*jai mes mia mi go*)
Jaime is my friend.

Vamos a la universidad.   (*va mo sa lau ni ver si dad*)
We're going to the university.

Fuimos de vacaciones en agosto.   (*fui mos de va ca cio ne se na <u>gos</u> to*)
We went on vacation in August.

If you practice reading and speaking in this manner, you will more easily understand spoken Spanish.

Don't Forget

Pronunciation is a skill that requires a lot of practice. Reading aloud is one of the best ways to do this.

Here are a few sentences to help you show off.

¿Cómo está usted?   (*co mwe stau <u>sted</u>*)
How are you?

¿De dónde es usted?   (*de don de su <u>sted</u>*)
Where are you from?

Vamos a comer.   (*va mo sa co <u>mer</u>*)
Let's go eat.

Es usted muy amable.   (*e su sted mu ia <u>ma</u> ble*)
You are very kind.

Esta ciudad es muy bonita.   (*e sta ciu da des muy bo <u>ni</u> ta*)
This city is very beautiful.

Me encanta hablar español.   (*meng can ta bla res pa <u>ñol</u>*)
I love to speak Spanish.

Beginning Spanish
for the Utterly CONFUSED

CHAPTER 1

Being Friendly

➡ Do I know how to say hello and good-bye to people in Spanish? If they are good friends, do I know what else I should do?

➡ Can I express "Good morning," "Good afternoon," and "Good night"? Am I sure about when these expressions are used?

➡ Do I know what to say if I leave a roomful of people?

➡ What about if I accidentally step on someone's foot?

➡ Is my pronunciation of the expressions for "please" and "thank you" correct?

➡ Do I know what to say when I am introduced to someone? Am I able to express congratulations for birthdays and other festive events?

➡ Can I welcome people to my home or my hometown?

➡ Do I know when to use ¡ ! and ¿ ?

Get Started

Here are some expressions that can be used to show politeness or to express feelings. Follow the pronunciation guidelines according to the explanations in Chapter 1.

To greet someone at any time of the day, evening, or night, you can say:

¡Hola! ¿Qué tal?　　(*o la que <u>tal</u>*)
Hi, how are you?

The response to this is

* to a good friend:
  Bien, gracias. ¿Y tú?　　(*byen gra cia si <u>tu</u>*)
  Fine, thanks. And you?

* to someone you do not normally socialize with:
  Bien, gracias. ¿Y usted?　　(*byen gra cia siu <u>sted</u>*)
  Fine, thanks. And you?

Quick Tip

When good friends meet and say good-bye, women normally touch cheeks and "kiss the air" (one [right] cheek in Latin America, both [right, then left] cheeks in Spain)—with both their male and female friends. Men look over each other's left shoulder and pat each other on the back, in an *abrazo*.

Don't Forget

Freeze your vowels!

To greet someone between daylight and lunchtime, say:

¡Buenos días!　　(*bue nos <u>di</u> as*)

Between lunchtime and darkness, say:

¡Buenas tardes!　　(*bue nas <u>tar</u> des*)

When it is dark, say:

¡Buenas noches!　　(*bue nas <u>no</u> ches*)

When you are introduced to someone, you can say:

Mucho gusto.   (*moo cho gu sto*)
I'm glad to meet you.

If the other person says **Mucho gusto** first, you can answer:

Igualmente.   (*ee ual men te*)
Likewise.

or: El gusto es mío.   (*el gu stwes mi o*)
The pleasure is mine.

or: Encantado (*if you are a male*).   (*eng can ta tho*)
I'm charmed.

Encantada (*if you are a female*).   (*eng can ta tha*)
I'm charmed.

To welcome people to your country, city, organization, or home, say:

(to one person, who is male)	Bienvenido	(*byen be ni tho*)
(to one person, who is female)	Bienvenida	(*byen be ni tha*)
(to several people)	Bienvenidos	(*byen be ni thos*)
(to a group of only females)	Bienvenidas	(*byen be ni thas*)

At **meals** or **parties:**

- Before a meal, say:
  ¡Buen provecho!   (*bwen pro be cho*)
  Enjoy your meal!

- To toast before drinking, say:
  ¡Salud!   (*sa lud*)
  To your health!

For **celebrations:**

¡Felicidades! (*fe li si tha thes*)
Congratulations!

¡Feliz cumpleaños! (*fe lis cum ple a nyos*)
Happy birthday!

¡Feliz Navidad! (*fe lis na bi thath*)
Merry Christmas!

¡Feliz Año Nuevo!   (*fe li sa nyo nwe bo*)
Happy New Year!

The following is good for any special day:

¡Feliz Día!   (*fe lis di a*)

For **politeness:**

Por favor.   (*por fa bor*)
Please.

Gracias.   (*gra syas*)
Thank you.

Muchas gracias.   (*mu chas gra syas*)
Thank you very much.

Muchísimas gracias.   (*mu chi si mas gra syas*)
Thanks a million.

De nada.   (*de na tha*)
You're welcome.

¡Perdón!   (*per don*)
Excuse me!

Con permiso.   (*con per mi so*)
Excuse me, I have to leave.

Lo siento mucho.   (*lo syen to mu cho*)
I'm very sorry.

In **emergencies:**

¡Cuidado!   (*kwi tha tho*)
Be careful!

¡Socorro!   (*so co rro*)
Help!

To **say good-bye:**

Hasta luego.   (*a stal weh go*)
See you later.

Hasta mañana.   (*a sta ma nya na*)
See you tomorrow.

Don't Forget

The "r" doesn't sound like an English *r*. Be sure to tap your tongue behind your top teeth.

nos vemos

<u>Nos vemos.</u>   (*nos <u>be</u> mos*)
See you soon.

Adiós.   (*ath <u>yos</u>*)
Good-bye.

Que le vaya bien.   (*ke le ba ya <u>byen</u>*)
May all go well with you.

Test Yourself

1.1 Look at the examples in this chapter and describe when ¡ and ! are used. Is one ever used without the other?

1.2 Look at the examples in this chapter and describe when ¿ and ? are used. Is one ever used without the other?

1.3 Write the Spanish equivalents of the following.

_____	_____	_____
Welcome, friends.	*Good evening.*	*Be careful.*
_____	_____	_____
Good morning.	*Enjoy your meal.*	*Excuse me. I'm leaving.*
_____	_____	_____
Thank you.	*Happy birthday.*	*To your health.*
_____	_____	_____
Oops—excuse me.	*Help!*	*Good afternoon.*
_____	_____	_____
Please.	*You're welcome.*	*Glad to meet you.*
_____	_____	_____
See you later.	*Good-bye.*	*May all go well with you.*

It's a Wrap

Practice saying these expressions to your Spanish-speaking friends, and say them aloud to yourself to get used to saying them automatically.

CHAPTER 2

Developing a Spanish Vocabulary

→ Do I know how to guess the meaning of words I hear and see in Spanish?

→ Do I know how English can help lead me to the Spanish word I want?

→ Do I know the best way to use a dictionary?

Get a jump-start on your Spanish vocabulary by realizing how many Spanish words you already know. A great number of words not only have similar spelling but also similar meaning in both Spanish and English. These are called cognates.

Let's look at a sample of cognates in each of the four categories of content words. Try to visualize each word as you pronounce it in Spanish. Follow the pronunciation guidelines in Chapter 1. To help you here, the most prominent syllable of each word is underlined. All of these words are pronounced for you on the recording. Listen to each one carefully, and then repeat it after the speaker.

Group 1: Nouns

ani<u>mal</u>	ho<u>tel</u>	<u>tren</u>	id<u>e</u>a
ac<u>tor</u>	<u>cen</u>tro	auto<u>bús</u>	informa<u>ción</u>
doc<u>tor</u>	<u>nor</u>te	bici<u>cle</u>ta	satisfac<u>ción</u>
profe<u>sor</u>	<u>es</u>te	motoci<u>cle</u>ta	crea<u>ción</u>
asis<u>ten</u>te	<u>oes</u>te	ar<u>tí</u>culo	reac<u>ción</u>
presi<u>den</u>te	conti<u>nen</u>te	te<u>lé</u>fono	dificul<u>tad</u>
resi<u>den</u>te	restau<u>ran</u>te	<u>trá</u>fico	facili<u>dad</u>
den<u>tis</u>ta	ofi<u>ci</u>na		responsabili<u>dad</u>
ar<u>tis</u>ta	hemis<u>fe</u>rio		
femi<u>nis</u>ta			
recepcio<u>nis</u>ta			
carpin<u>te</u>ro			

Group 2: Adjectives

princi<u>pal</u>	perma<u>nen</u>te	crea<u>ti</u>vo
natu<u>ral</u>	fasci<u>nan</u>te	ac<u>ti</u>vo
di<u>fí</u>cil	ele<u>gan</u>te	atrac<u>ti</u>vo
popu<u>lar</u>	impor<u>tan</u>te	mo<u>der</u>no
	intere<u>san</u>te	fa<u>mo</u>so
	ho<u>rri</u>ble	fan<u>tás</u>tico
	so<u>cia</u>ble	compli<u>ca</u>do

Group 3: Verbs

expre<u>sar</u>	prome<u>ter</u>	deci<u>dir</u>
conver<u>sar</u>	estable<u>cer</u>	defi<u>nir</u>
invi<u>tar</u>	defen<u>der</u>	reci<u>bir</u>
acep<u>tar</u>	sorpren<u>der</u>	ocu<u>rrir</u>
fasci<u>nar</u>		
concen<u>trar</u>		
anun<u>ciar</u>		

Group 4: Adverbs

rá<u>pido</u>	rá<u>pidamente</u>
silen<u>cioso</u>	silenciosa<u>mente</u>
	prá<u>cticamente</u>
	especial<u>mente</u>
	principal<u>mente</u>
	evidente<u>mente</u>

Use cognates to help build your vocabulary of *content words,* but not *function words.* Think of the function words as part of a stable framework, and the content words as substitutable blocks that fit into it. Sometimes we can find a cognate by thinking of the English word we would *write* rather than one we would say in informal conversation. We often use words with Latin origins in our more formal English expression. For example, the word *say* doesn't give us any clues to finding a Spanish word; however, if we think *express,* it leads us straight to **expresar**. Likewise, *talk* doesn't help us, but *converse* gives us **conversar**.

There is one caution. False cognates, also known as **falsos amigos,** are the basis of many jokes and the subject of a number of dictionaries. These are words that do indeed look alike in both languages but that have quite different, sometimes even opposite, meanings. A good example, and perhaps the most potentially embarrassing **falso amigo,** is the following: **embarazada** looks an awful lot like *embarrassed,* but it means *pregnant.* The most common of these **falsos amigos** will be pointed out in this book in the course of the lessons.

Using the Dictionary

Throughout this book you will be given instructions to use a Spanish-English dictionary to find the content words you personally need. At that time you will have a good understanding of how those words are used to express the meaning you want. In other words, look up content words when you know how to use and change them.

At this point, try to avoid looking up function words. You will have a much more natural feeling for these words and expressions if you learn them in the context of the dialogues presented in the lessons.

CHAPTER 3

Identifying People

Do I Need to Read This Chapter?

➡ Can I ask people their names, their friends' and family members' names, where they are from, and what they do?

➡ Can I tell people who I am, what country and what area of the country I'm from, and what I do for a living?

➡ Do I know the difference between **soy** and **yo soy**?

➡ Do I know when to say **señora García** and when to say **la señora García**?

➡ Do I know how to make a yes-or-no question in Spanish?

➡ Do I know how to make nouns plural?

To Say Who You Are in Spanish

The verb **ser** is the most common verb in Spanish, and it is used here to tell who people are and where they are from.

Forms of the Verb *ser*

soy	es	es	es	es
I am	*you are*	*he is*	*she is*	*it is*

Get Started

1. Read the dialogue several times.

2. With a small card, cover up the Spanish questions and see if you can remember how to say them, using the English questions as a cue. Do the same with the answers. Then cover up the Spanish answers and see if you can answer each question. Finally, cover up the answers and see if you can make the corresponding question.

3. After you have done this silently and checked your answers, listen to the dialogue on the recording as you read it silently in the book. Then play it again, pausing after each sentence in order to repeat it.

4. Do the same exercise in written form, paying attention to the punctuation, especially the upside-down question marks and the accent marks.

Dialogue 1 🔘

Jorge	Margarita
¿Quién es él? *Who is he?*	Es mi amigo. *He's my friend.*
¿Cuál es su nombre? *What's his name?*	Su nombre es Juan. *His name is Juan.*
¿De dónde es? *Where is he from?*	Es de Perú./Es del Perú. *He's from Peru.*

Quién
キーン
= who.

Jorge	Margarita
Perdón, ¿cuál es su nombre? ¿Es usted María?	No, no soy María. Soy Margarita. Mi nombre es Margarita.
Excuse me, what's your name? *Are you Maria?*	*No, I'm not Maria, I'm Margarita.* *My name is Margarita.*
¿Es usted de Perú?	No, no soy de Perú, sino de Bolivia.
Are you from Peru?	*No, I'm not from Peru; I'm from Bolivia.*
¿Quién es María?	Ella es María. Su nombre es María.
Who is Maria?	*She's Maria. Her name is Maria.*
Es de Perú, ¿verdad?	Sí, ella es de Perú, pero yo no.
She's from Peru, isn't she?	*Yes, she's from Peru, but I'm not.*

What *Is* the Difference between *soy* and *yo soy*?

How can we know who someone is talking about if **es** means *you are, he is, she is,* and *it is*? If it isn't already clear, we can use *subject pronouns* to clarify or emphasize who we are talking about.

yo	usted	él	ella	él/ella
I	*you*	*he*	*she*	*it*

¿Es usted María?	No, no soy María. Ella es María.
Are you Maria?	*No, I'm not Maria. She's Maria.*
¿Quién es Margarita?	Yo soy Margarita.
Who is Margarita?	*I'm Margarita.*

主語のいらない！

Quick Tip

Using a subject pronoun in Spanish is like setting the word in boldface type in English, or saying it a little bit louder for emphasis. Remember: only use the subject pronoun when it is necessary for clarification.

To Say *my*, *your*, *his*, and *her*

Test Yourself

3.1 If you have learned the dialogue, you should be able to write these *possessive pronouns*. If you are not sure, go back and review the dialogue.

_____ nombre   _____ nombre   _____ nombre   _____ nombre
my   *your*   *her*   *his*

_____ amigo/a   _____ amigo/a   _____ amigo/a   _____ amigo/a
my   *your*   (*her*) *su*   *his*

To Ask a Question in Spanish

3.2 If you have learned the dialogue, you should be able to write these *interrogative* words. Be sure to include the question marks and the accent marks. Review the dialogue to make sure you know where they go.

Who . . . ? _____

From where . . . ? _____

What is . . . ? _____

Statement: Usted es de Honduras.
   You're from Honduras.

Question: ¿Usted es de Honduras? / ¿Es usted de Honduras?
   Are you from Honduras?

To Make a Sentence Negative

3.3 Look at Dialogue 1 and then answer these questions.

How do you say *no* in Spanish? _____

How do you say *not*? _____

3.4 Answer each of the following questions in a complete sentence.

¿Quién es usted? ¿Cuál es su nombre?

¿De dónde es usted?

¿Quién es su amigo/a?

¿De dónde es él/ella?

3.5 Form a question for each of the following answers.

Su nombre es Ana.

Mi amigo es Francisco.

Es de Bolivia.

Soy de México.

No, no soy de España.

Check your answers with the Answer Key in the Appendix.

It's a Wrap

Now you can ask and answer important personal questions. Practice doing this by talking to yourself aloud—and any time you get the opportunity in a real-life situation.

To Identify People by General Category

el   la

Observe the following nouns that name people.

Male	Female
el hombre	la mujer
man	*woman*
el muchacho	la muchacha
boy	*girl*
el chico	la chica
boy	*girl*
el niño	la niña
male child	*female child*
el amigo	la amiga
male friend	*female friend*
el vecino	la vecina
male neighbor	*female neighbor*
el señor	la señora
gentleman	*lady*
el español	la española
Spaniard	*Spaniard*

3.6 Now describe the patterns by filling in the blanks.

The words that indicate males are preceded by _____ .

The words that indicate females are preceded by _____ .

The words that end in a consonant for males add _____ for females.

The words that end in **o** for males usually end in _____ for females.

To Identify Someone by Nationality

Following are nouns that indicate various nationalities. Observe their endings.

el español / la española *Spaniard*	el mexicano / la mexicana *Mexican*
el inglés / la inglesa *English citizen*	el cubano / la cubana *Cuban*
el francés / la francesa *French citizen*	el dominicano / la dominicana *Dominican*
el alemán / la alemana *German citizen*	el peruano / la peruana *Peruvian*
	el venezolano / la venezolana *Venezuelan*
el estadounidense / la estadounidense *U.S. citizen*	el colombiano / la colombiana *Colombian*
el canadiense / la canadiense *Canadian*	el ecuatoriano / la ecuatoriana *Ecuadoran*
el nicaragüense / la nicaragüense *Nicaraguan*	el boliviano / la boliviana *Bolivian*
el costarricense / la costarricense *Costa Rican*	el hondureño / la hondureña *Honduran*
	el salvadoreño / la salvadoreña *Salvadoran*
	el panameño / la panameña *Panamanian*

el puertorriqueño / la puertorriqueña
Puerto Rican

el guatemalteco / la guatemalteca
Guatemalan

el chileno / la chilena
Chilean

el argentino / la argentina
Argentine

el uruguayo / la uruguaya
Uruguayan

el paraguayo / la paraguaya
Paraguayan

3.7 Now write the pattern.

The nouns that end in a consonant for males add _____ for females.

The nouns that end in **o** for males end in _____ for females.

The nouns that end in **e** for males end in _____ for females.

The names for nationalities begin with a _____ *el* _____ letter.

3.8 Complete the chart.

Male	Female
el mexicano	_____
_____	la costarricense
el guatemalteco	_____
_____	la chilena
el señor	_____
_____	la estadounidense
	la española
el niño	_____
_____	la hondureña

Do Nouns Name Only People? What About Places and Objects? How Can They Be Masculine or Feminine?

Nouns also name places, objects, and abstract ideas. Even though these are not male or female, the word that names each one is either of masculine or feminine gender.

Observe the following nouns that name places.

Masculino		Femenino
el país *country*	el norte *north*	la nación *nation*
el estado *state*	el sur *south*	la ciudad *city*
el pueblo *town*	el este *east*	la capital *capital*
el barrio *neighborhood*	el oeste *west*	la vecindad *neighborhood*
el campo *countryside*	el centro *middle*	la parte *area*
el lugar *place*		

3.9 Fill in the blanks.

Each noun is of one of _____ types, or genders (not sexes).

Masculine nouns are preceded by _____ .

Feminine nouns are preceded by _____ .

Quick Tip

The best way to remember the gender of a noun is to learn the article—*el* or *la*—and the new word at the same time. Think *el norte* rather than just *norte.*

Quick Tip

It's the word, not the object, that belongs to a gender. Sometimes an object can have more than one name—and the names may be of different genders, for example, *el país / la nación; el barrio / la vecindad.*

To Find Out What Part of the Country Someone Is From

Get Started

Learn the dialogue by following the same procedures suggested for learning Dialogue 1.

Dialogue 2

Marta	Roberto
¿Su profesor de español es el Sr. López?	No. Mi profesora es la Sra. González.
Is Mr. Lopez your Spanish teacher?	*No, Mrs. Gonzalez is my teacher.*
¿De qué país es?	Es de España.
What country is she from?	*She's from Spain.*
¿Ah, sí? ¿De qué ciudad es?	Es de Madrid, la capital.
Really? What city is she from?	*She's from Madrid, the capital.*
Bueno, el Sr. López es de España también, pero no es de Madrid.	¿De qué parte es?
Well, Mr. Lopez is from Spain, too, but he's not from Madrid.	*What area is he from?*
Es del sur del país.	¡Qué interesante!
He's from the south of the country.	*That's interesting!*

Quick Tips

señor (*se <u>nyor</u>*), the equivalent of *Mr.,* is abbreviated **Sr.**
señora (*se <u>nyo</u> ra*), the equivalent of *Mrs.,* is abbreviated **Sra.**
señorita (*se nyo <u>ri</u> ta*), the equivalent of *Miss,* is abreviated **Srta.**

When speaking directly to someone you normally address with a title, say:

¡Buenos días, **Sr.** López!   ¡Hola, **Sra.** González!

¡Buenas tardes, **Dr.** Díaz!   ¿Es usted de Perú, **Srta.** Martínez?

When talking about someone with a title, add **el** or **la.**

Mi profesor es **el señor** López.   Mi profesora es **la señora** González.

El médico es **el doctor** Díaz.   Su amiga es **la señorita** Martínez.

El señor López es del sur.   **La señora** González es de Madrid.

Quick Tip

de + el = del

Compare the following:

la ciudad   Susana es **de la** ciudad de Chicago.

el estado   Raúl es **del** estado de California.

el norte   Marta es **del** norte de México.

3.10 Review the dialogue if necessary, then fill in the blanks.

*Choose **de la** or **del:***

El Dr. Díaz es _____ capital.

Soy _____ norte _____ país.

La Srta. Martínez no es _____ norte. Es _____ ciudad de México.

Write in your **Vocabulario personal** the nouns you have learned that are meaning-ful to you. For example, if you have a friend from **Perú,** include **peruano/a** in your list. If you need to talk about places and nationalities that are not here, look them up in your dictionary, note what categories they belong to, and add them to your list. Add others as you need them. Be sure to include the article (**el** or **la**) with each entry.

3.11 Answer the questions in complete sentences.

¿Cuál es su nombre?

¿De dónde es usted?

¿Es usted del norte del país?

¿Quién es su amigo?

¿De qué país es?

¿De qué ciudad es?

3.12 Form a question that corresponds to each answer.

El señor es mi amigo.

La Sra. Bravo es del sur de España.

Su nombre es Ester.

No, no es de la capital.

Sí, soy de Argentina.

No, no soy de Buenos Aires.

Talking to or About More than One Person

Get Started

Observe the plural forms of the verb *ser.*

somos	son	son
we are	*you all are*	*they are*

Now look at the plural subject pronouns.

Don't Forget

Just like the singular subject pronouns, plural subject pronouns are used only for clarification or emphasis:

nosotros	nosotras
we	*we girls / we women*

ustedes
you all / you guys / all of you

ellos	ellas
they	*they (when all are female)*

Learn the following dialogue by following the procedures suggested for learning Dialogue 1.

Dialogue 3

el Sr. Bravo	Ana y Beatriz
Perdón, ¿quiénes son ustedes?	Somos Ana y Beatriz.
Excuse me, who are you all?	*We're Ana and Beatriz.*
¿Son hermanas?	Sí, somos hermanas.
Are you sisters?	*Yes, we're sisters.*

el Sr. Bravo	Ana y Beatriz
¿Cuáles son sus apellidos? *What are your last names?*	Nuestro primer apellido es Hernández y el segundo es García. *Our first last name is Hernandez, and the second one is Garcia.*
Ustedes son de Colombia, ¿verdad? *You're from Colombia, aren't you?*	Sí, somos de Bogotá. ¿Por qué? *Yes, we're from Bogota. Why?*
Y sus padres son Germán y Berta, ¿no es así? *And your parents are German and Berta, right?*	Sí, así es. Pero, ¿quién es usted? *That's right. But who are you?*
Soy José Fernández Bravo. Sus padres son mis buenos amigos. *I'm Jose Fernandez Bravo. Your parents are good friends of mine.*	¡Increíble! ¡Qué casualidad! Las hijas de usted son nuestras compañeras de clase. *Unbelievable! What a coincidence! Your daughters are our classmates.*

To Make Nouns Plural

Observe the following.

Masculino		Femenino	
Singular	**Plural**	**Singular**	**Plural**
el hombre	los hombres	la parte	las partes
el amigo	los amigos	la amiga	las amigas
el español	los españoles	la española	las españolas
el inglés	los ingleses	la inglesa	las inglesas
el lugar	los lugares	la mujer	las mujeres
		la vecindad	las vecindades

3.13 Now write the patterns.

To make a noun plural:

add _____ if it ends in a consonant.

add _____ if it ends in a vowel.

change **el** to _____ .

change **la** to _____ .

3.14 Complete the following chart.

Singular	Plural
el nombre	_____
_____	los profesores
_____	las mexicanas
la uruguaya	_____
_____	los paraguayos
el barrio	_____
_____	las peruanas
la ciudad	_____
_____	los lugares
la nación*	_____
_____	las vecindades
el estado	_____
_____	las amigas
_____	los vecinos

*When a syllable is added to a word that has a **tilde** (written accent mark) on the final syllable, the **tilde** is dropped.

Observe the following sentences.

One friend	*More than one friend*
Mi amigo es Juan.	Mis amigos son Juan y Pedro.
My friend is Juan.	*My friends are Juan and Pedro.*
Su amigo es Carlos.	Sus amigos son Carlos y Pepe.
His friend is Carlos.	*His friends are Carlos and Pepe.*

Ana es su amiga también.
Ana is his friend, too.

Ana y Rosy son sus amigas también.
Ana and Rosy are his friends, too.

El profesor es nuestro amigo.
The teacher is our friend.

Los profesores son nuestros amigos.
The teachers are our friends.

La señora es nuestra amiga.
The lady is our friend.

Las señoras son nuestras amigas.
The ladies are our friends.

3.15 Now describe the patterns.

If what I have is singular, *my* = _____ .

If what I have is plural, *my* = _____ .

If what you, he, she, or they have is singular, *your, his, her,* and *their* = _____ .

If what you, he, she, or they have is plural, *your, his, her,* and *their* = _____ .

In other words, if the word following the possessive pronoun ends in **s,** the possessive pronoun ends in _____ .

3.16 Write in the possessive pronouns.

_____ apellido   _____ nombres   _____ amigo   _____ padres
my   *your*   *his*   *her*

_____ apellidos   _____ nombre   _____ amigos   _____ padre
their   *my*   *your*   *his*

Don't Forget

**Review the words
that ask questions.**

3.17 Write the questions in the blanks. Remember your question marks and accent marks. Look at the dialogues if necessary.

Who . . . ? _____

Who . . . ? _____ (when you think the answer is plural)

From what country . . . ? _____

From what city . . . ? _____

From what area . . . ? _____

3.18 Practice answering the following questions in complete sentences; then listen to them on the recording, pausing it to answer them again. After you have given your answer, a speaker will give his own personal answer, which will probably not be exactly like yours. Other acceptable answers are given in the Answer Key in the Appendix.

¿De qué país es usted?

¿Es usted del centro del país?

¿De qué ciudad es su mejor amigo?

¿Son de Chile sus vecinos?

3.19 Form a question for each of the following answers.

Es de Bolivia.

Sí, somos de La Paz.

No, no es de Uruguay.

Son de la costa de Perú.

Soy de la ciudad de México.

It's a Wrap

Suggestions for further practice.

1. Talk to yourself. Ask and answer questions such as, "Where am I from?" and "Where are my friends from?"

2. Ask your Spanish-speaking friends what country, city, or area they are from. Tell them the same information about yourself. Write down the information they give you. And tell them to stay tuned—you'll be back with more questions next week.

La familia

LOS GARCÍA
the García family

El Sr. García	La Sra. (de)* García
Pedro García Márquez	María González de García
don Pedro	doña María
el esposo de María	**la esposa** de Pedro
el padre de José y Ana	**la madre** de José y Ana
el suegro de Elena y de Raúl	**la suegra** de Elena y de Raúl
el abuelo de Luisa, Juan, Juana y Jorge	**la abuela** de Luisa, Juan, Juana y Jorge

LOS GARCÍA   **LOS HERNÁNDEZ**

La Sra. (de) García	El Sr. García	La Sra. (de) Hernández	El Sr. Hernández
Elena Díaz Gómez	José García González	Ana García González	Raúl Hernández Castro
la nuera de Pedro y María	**el hijo** de Pedro y María	**la hija** de Pedro y María	**el yerno** de Pedro y María
	el hermano de Ana	**la hermana** de José	
la esposa de José	**el esposo** de Elena	**la esposa** de Raúl	**el esposo** de Ana
la cuñada de Ana	**el cuñado** de Raúl	**la cuñada** de Elena	**el cuñado** de José
la madre de Luisa y Juan	**el padre** de Luisa y Juan	**la madre** de Juana y Jorge	**el padre** de Juana y Jorge
la tía de Juana y Jorge	**el tío** de Juana y Jorge	**la tía** de Luisa y Juan	**el tío** de Luisa y Juan

Luisa García Díaz	Juan García Díaz	Juana Hernández García	Jorge Hernández García
la hija de Elena y José	**el hijo** de Elena y José	**la hija** de Ana y Raúl	**el hijo** de Ana y Raúl
la hermana de Juan	**el hermano** de Luisa	**la hermana** de Jorge	**el hermano** de Juana
la nieta de Pedro y María	**el nieto** de Pedro y María	**la nieta** de Pedro y María	**el nieto** de Pedro y María
la sobrina de Ana y Raúl	**el sobrino** de Ana y Raúl	**la sobrina** de Elena y José	**el sobrino** de Elena y José
la prima de Juana y Jorge	**el primo** de Juana y Jorge	**la prima** de Luisa y Juan	**el primo** de Luisa y Juan

***de** is optional here.

Get Started

Observe carefully the family tree in the accompanying figure.

3.20 Now write in the Spanish equivalents. (Don't forget **el** or **la**.)

grandfather	*abuelo*	grandmother	*abuela*
grandson	*nieto*	granddaughter	*nieta*
father	*padre*	mother	*madre*
son	*hijo*	daughter	*hija*
brother	~~ermano~~ *ermano*	sister	*ermana*
uncle	*nieto*	aunt	*nieta*
nephew	*sobrino*	niece	*sobrina*
boy cousin	*primo*	girl cousin	*prime*
father-in-law		mother-in-law	
brother-in-law		sister-in-law	

How Do You Say _____'s in Spanish?

You don't!

Observe the following examples.

Pedro no es mi padre. Pedro es el padre de José.

Elena no es la esposa de Raúl. Es la esposa de José.

Luisa y Juan no son los hijos de Ana. Son los hijos de Elena.

3.21 Now write the pattern.

There is no *'s* in Spanish. To express *José's father,* you say:

_____

Quick Tips

parientes = *relatives*
padres = *parents*

Observe the following.

el hermano + el hermano = los hermanos

la hermana + la hermana = las hermanas

el hermano + la hermana = los hermanos

el padre + la madre = los padres

3.22 Now write the pattern.

When all the members of a group are male, the plural is <u>masculine</u>.

When all the members of a group are female, the plural is _feminine_ .

If there is at least one male in the group, the plural is _masculine_

3.23 Look at the first example, then complete the chart.

Pedro es el abuelo de Juana. María es la abuela de Juana.	Pedro y María son los abuelos de Juana.
Pedro es el padre de Ana. María es la madre de Ana.	_____
José es el hijo de Pedro. Ana es la hija de Pedro.	_____
_____ _____	Elena y José son los tíos de Jorge.
_____ _____	Juana y Jorge son los primos de Luisa.
_____ _____	Luisa y Juana son las nietas de María.
Luisa es la sobrina de Ana. Susana es la sobrina de Ana.	_____

3.24 Look at the example, then answer the question.

¿Quién es Jorge?	Es el hijo de Ana y Raúl, el hermano de Juana, el nieto de Pedro y María, el sobrino de Elena y José y el primo de Luisa y Juan.

¿Quién es usted en su familia?

What Are *Novios?*

Los novios are sweethearts. **La novia** can be anyone from a steady girlfriend to a fiancée to a bride. The bride and groom are **los novios** until after the wedding ceremony; then they are **los recién casados**—the newlyweds.

Why Do People Have <u>Two Last Names</u> in Spanish?

The Spanish naming system is a unique way to recognize the mother's maiden name for one more generation. The first last name (**el primer apellido**) is the father's family name. The second last name (**el segundo apellido**) is the mother's maiden name.

When: Juan Martínez González   marries   Juana Rojas Rodríguez
(El Sr. Martínez)

She becomes: Juana Rojas de Martínez
[La Sra. (de) Martínez]

Their son's name is David Martínez Rojas.

Their daughter's name is María Martínez Rojas.

Titles are used with the first **apellido** or with both, but not with just the second one. For example, **María Martínez Rojas** could be **la señorita Martínez** or **la señorita Martínez Rojas,** but not **la señorita Rojas.**

Write your name according to the Spanish system. _____

What is your title? _____

It's a Wrap   Add your new nouns to your **Vocabulario personal** on p. 235.

Another Way to Say *You*

When you are talking to your family members or close friends—people you generally socialize with—you will want to address them as **tú** rather than **usted,** which is used with people with whom you have a more formal relationship.

tú	eres	tú eres	tu
you	*you are*	<u>*you*</u> *are*	*your*

Look at these examples.

¿Cuál es tu nombre?   Mi nombre es Jorge.
What's your name?   *My name is Jorge.*

¿De dónde eres?   Soy de Venezuela.
Where are you from?   *I'm from Venezuela.*

¿Cuáles son tus apellidos?   Mis apellidos son Martínez y Gómez.
What are your last names?   *My last names are Martinez and Gomez.*

When people get to know each other, they often ask for permission to use **tú.**

¿Nos tuteamos?
*May we use **tú** with each other?*

Are There Any Other Ways of Saying *You*?

Yes, but it would be confusing and counterproductive to learn them at this point. For example, in Argentina and Central America, very close friends use **vos** and its corresponding verb forms as an alternative to **tú**. You will need this form of address only if you decide to spend a lot of time in one of these areas, although everybody in these countries understands, and also uses, **tú.**

In Spain, almost everyone uses an additional plural, **vosotros/as,** and its corresponding verb forms as the plural for **tú**—and **ustedes** as the plural only for **usted**. In Latin America, however, **ustedes** is universally the plural for both **tú** and **usted**. To avoid confusion, the **ustedes** form is used throughout this book. Notes on **vosotros** and the verb forms used with it are listed in the Appendix.

Ahora, ¿nos tuteamos?

From now on, the questions addressed to you in this book will be in the **tú** form.

Jobs and Professions

To Find Out What Somebody Does for a Living

Get Started

Learn the dialogue by following the same procedures suggested for learning Dialogue 1.

Dialogue 4 *En una recepción para médicos.*

Ángeles	Carolina
Hola, soy Ángeles. Soy la esposa del Dr. Páez.	Encantada. Mi nombre es Carolina. Soy médico. Todos aquí somos médicos, ¿verdad?
Hi, I'm Angeles. I'm Dr. Paez's wife.	*How nice to meet you. My name is Carolina. I'm a doctor. We're all doctors, aren't we?*
No, no soy médico, sino abogada. Mi esposo es cardiólogo. ¿Cuál es la profesión de su esposo?	Es médico también, ginecólogo.
No, I'm not a doctor. I'm a lawyer. My husband is a cardiologist. What does your husband do?	*He's a doctor, too—a gynecologist.*
¿Quién es el otro señor? Cuál es su especialidad?	Es el Dr. Chávez. Es profesor de medicina.
Who is the other gentleman? What is his specialization?	*That's Dr. Chavez. He's a professor of medicine.*
Ah sí, claro. Mis hijos son sus estudiantes. Los dos son estudiantes de medicina.	¿De verdad? Mi hija es estudiante de medicina también.
Oh yes, of course. My sons are his students. They're both medical students.	*Really? My daughter is a medical student, too.*

3.25 Answer the questions about the dialogue.

¿Quién es Ángeles?

¿Cuál es su profesión?

¿Cuál es la profesión de los esposos de Ángeles y Carolina?

¿Cuál es la profesión de Carolina?

¿Cuál es la especialidad de su esposo?

¿Quiénes son estudiantes?

¿Quién es su profesor?

Names of Typical Jobs and Professions

Study the following chart, and observe the endings of the nouns.

Masculino			Femenino		
(el) artista	comentar**ista**	period**ista**	**(la) artista**	comentar**ista**	period**ista**
(*the*) *artist*	*commentator*	*journalist*	(*the*) *artist*	*commentator*	*journalist*
dent**ista**	ten**ista**	futbol**ista**	dent**ista**	ten**ista**	futbol**ista**
dentist	*tennis player*	*soccer player*	*dentist*	*tennis player*	*soccer player*
pian**ista**			pian**ista**		
piano player			*piano player*		
(el) estudiante	cant**ante**	ag**ente**	**(la) estudiante**	cant**ante**	ag**ente**
(*the*) *student*	*singer*	*agent*	(*the*) *student*	*singer*	*agent*
ger**ente**	client**e**	dependient**e**	ger**ente**	client**e**	dependient**e**
manager	*customer*	*store clerk*	*manager*	*customer*	*store clerk*
ayudant**e**	jef**e**	asistent**e** social	ayudant**e**	jef**a***	asistent**e** social
assistant	*boss*	*social worker*	*assistant*	*boss*	*social worker*
(el) profesor	escrit**or**	contad**or**	**(la) profesora**	escrit**ora**	contad**ora**
(*the*) *teacher*	*writer*	*accountant*	(*the*) *teacher*	*writer*	*accountant*
direct**or**	vended**or**		direct**ora**	vended**ora**	
director	*salesman*		*director*	*saleswoman*	
programad**or**	diseñad**or**		programad**ora**	diseñad**ora**	
programmer	*designer*		*programmer*	*designer*	
act**or**			act**riz**		
actor			*actress*		

***la jefa** has become standard for *female boss*. In some places, you will also hear **la presidenta** and **la médica**.

Masculino			Femenino		
(el) polic**í**a *(the) policeman*	guía *guide*		**(la)** polic**í**a *(the) policewoman*	guía *guide*	
(el) alumn**o** *(the) pupil*	carter**o** *mailman*	secretari**o** *secretary*	**(la)** alumn**a** *(the) pupil*	carter**a** *mail carrier*	secretari**a** *secretary*
enfermer**o** *nurse*	maestr**o** *teacher*	consejer**o** *advisor*	enfermer**a** *nurse*	maestr**a** *teacher*	consejer**a** *advisor*
ingenier**o** *engineer*	abogad**o** *lawyer*	técnic**o** *technician*	ingenier**a** *engineer*	abogad**a** *lawyer*	técnic**a** *technician*
(el) model**o** *(the) model*	pilot**o** *piloto*	médic**o** *medical doctor*	**(la)** model**o** *(the) model*	pilot**o** *pilot*	médic**o** *medical doctor*

3.26 Now write the patterns.

The endings **ista** and **e** refer to both men and women. The difference is indicated by the use of _____ or _____ before the word. If the name of a male's profession ends in **or,** the female counterpart ends in _____; the one common exception is _____. If the name of the profession ends in **ía,** it refers to a _____ or a _____. If the name of the profession ends in **o** for a male, it ends in _____ for female; the three exceptions are _____, _____, and _____.

It's a Wrap

Add to your **Vocabulario personal** the names of the jobs and professions of the people who are important to you. Look up in your dictionary the ones not listed here; decide which category they belong to, then add them to your list.

Learn the following dialogue, taking the usual steps.

Dialogue 5 🔘

Luisa	Octavia
¿Quién es Julio Ochoa? *Who is Julio Ochoa?*	Es el profesor. *He's the teacher.*
¿Quién es Fernanda López? *Who is Fernanda Lopez?*	Es la secretaria del jefe del departamento. *She's the secretary to the head of the department.*

Luisa	Octavia
¿Quiénes son Pablo Ruiz e Ignacio Reyes?	Son los abogados de mi vecino.
Who are Pablo Ruiz and Ignacio Reyes?	*They're my neighbor's lawyers.*
¿Es médico su vecino?	No, no es médico, sino arquitecto.
Is your neighbor a doctor?	*No, he's not a doctor; he's an architect.*
Y usted, ¿es camarera?	No, no soy camarera, sino estudiante.
Are you a waitress?	*No, I'm not a waitress; I'm a student.*
¿Cuál es el trabajo de su novio?	Es cocinero.
What does your boyfriend do?	*He's a cook.*
¿Son cocineras Ana e Irma?	No, no son cocineras. Son camareras.
Are Ana and Irma cooks?	*No, they're not cooks; they're waitresses.*

3.27 Look at the following sentences, then write the pattern.

Ana es ingeniera y profesora. Ana es profesora e ingeniera.

Irma y Berta son modelos. Berta e Irma son modelos.

Ignacio y Pablo son abogados. Pablo e Ignacio son abogados.

Y means _____ . **Y** changes to **e** before _____ .

3.28 Observe the following sentences, then follow the pattern.

Mi vecino no es médico. Es arquitecto.

Mi vecino no es médico, sino arquitecto.

Ana y Berta no son cocineras. Son camareras.

Ana y Berta no son cocineras, _____ camareras.

Now answer the following question.

¿Eres profesor(a) de español?

_____

Observe the following:

Gustavo es médico. Gustavo es el médico de José.
Gustavo is a doctor. *Gustavo is Jose's doctor.*

Julia es profesora. Julia es la profesora de mi hijo.
Julia is a teacher. *Julia is my son's teacher.*

Marcos es abogado.   Marcos es el abogado de mi vecino.
Marcos is a lawyer.   *Marcos is my neighbor's lawyer.*

3.29 Answer the following questions, following the model.

¿Quién es Gustavo?   Gustavo es el médico de José.

¿Cuál es el trabajo de Gustavo?   Gustavo es médico.

¿Quién es Julia?   _____

¿Cuál es el trabajo de Julia?   _____

¿Quién es Marcos?   _____

¿Cuál es el trabajo de Marcos?   _____

3.30 Practice answering the following questions in complete sentences; then listen to them on the recording, pausing it to answer them again. After you have given your answer, a speaker will give his own personal answer, which will probably not be exactly like yours. Other acceptable answers are given in the Answer Key in the Appendix.

 ¿Quién eres?

¿De dónde eres?

¿Cuál es tu profesión/trabajo?

¿Cuál es el nombre de tu amigo/a?

¿De dónde es?

¿Cuál es su profesión?

¿Quiénes son dos personas en tu familia?

¿Son tus primos?

¿De qué parte del país son?

¿Son de la ciudad o del campo?

3.31 Make up questions that are answered by the following.

No, no soy Manolo.

Sara es del centro del país.

Sí, somos nicaragüenses.

José y Juan son ingenieros.

No, Enrique no es su padre, sino su tío.

Sí, Marcos es nuestro hermano.

CHAPTER 4

Describing People

➡ Do I know how to interview someone and find out if he or she has the qualities I am looking for in, for example, an employee or a roommate?

➡ Am I able to describe myself to a potential employer or other important contact?

➡ Do I know how to write a good evaluation or recommendation about someone I know well?

➡ Do I know how to obtain or give a good description of doctors, lawyers, teachers, and others who provide services in the community?

➡ Could I describe my new boyfriend or girlfriend (or somebody else's) to my friends?

Get Started

Read and learn all of Ana's part in the following dialogue, then do the same with Beatriz's answer. Listen to the dialogue on the recording as you read it in the book. Then play it again, pausing after each sentence in order to repeat it.

Dialogue 6

Ana

Oye, Beatriz —tengo un anuncio interesante del periódico: # 4567 Nuevo en la ciudad
Listen, Beatriz—I have an interesting ad from the newspaper: #4567 New in town

"Soy un hombre soltero, de 36 años, medio alto, atlético.
"I'm a single man, 36 years old, medium height, athletic.

Tengo el pelo castaño y los ojos azules.
I have brown hair and blue eyes.

Soy dueño de mi propio negocio exitoso.
I own my own successful business.

Soy culto, serio y responsable, pero también divertido.
I am educated, serious, and responsible, but fun.

Tengo muchos intereses.
I have a lot of interests.

¿Cómo eres tú?
What are you like?

Si eres soltera, atractiva, vivaz pero no viva, si tienes una sonrisa bonita y si no eres muy alta —eres la mujer perfecta para mí."
If you are single, attractive, lively but not manipulative, if you have a pretty smile and if you're not too tall—you are the perfect woman for me."

Beatriz

Bueno, Ana —sí, es verdad que es un anuncio interesante.
Well, Ana—yes, it really is an interesting ad.

Ana

A ver, ¿cómo eres tú?
Let's see—what are you like?

Eres soltera y atractiva y tienes una sonrisa preciosa.
You're single and attractive and you have a beautiful smile.

Eres baja y tienes una personalidad muy agradable.
You're short and you have a very pleasant personality.

También tienes 36 años y tienes un buen trabajo.
You are 36, too, and you have a good job.

Beatriz

Pero mira —éste no es el periódico de hoy.
But look—this isn't today's paper.

Es un periódico viejo.
It's an old newspaper.

Ya es demasiado tarde.
Now it's too late.

◇ Test Yourself

4.1 Write in the blanks the words that describe the writer of the ad.

_____	_____	_____	_____
single	*athletic*	*successful*	*well educated*

_____	_____	_____
serious	*responsible*	*fun*

4.2 Write the words that describe the kind of woman he is looking for.

_____	_____	_____	_____
single	*attractive*	*vivacious* (*lively*)	*not too tall*

The words you wrote in the blanks are adjectives—content words that describe nouns. They answer questions like the following.

¿Cómo es usted? / ¿Cómo eres?
What are you like?

¿Cómo es tu hermano? / ¿Cómo es él?
What is your brother like? / What is he like?

¿Cómo es la profesora? / ¿Cómo es ella?
What is the teacher like? / What is she like?

¿Cómo son ustedes?
What are you all like?

¿Cómo son tus padres? / ¿Cómo son ellos?
What are your parents like? / What are they like?

More Adjectives That Describe People

Masculino/Femenino		Masculino/Femenino	Masculino/Femenino
(im)paciente *(im)patient*	adorable *adorable*	egoísta *selfish*	audaz *bold*
independiente *independent*	agradable *pleasant*	idealista *idealistic*	capaz *capable*
inteligente *intelligent*	amable *nice, kind*	machista *chauvinistic*	vivaz *lively*
persistente *persistent*	amigable *friendly*	materialista *materialistic*	joven *young*
exigente *strict*	responsable *responsible*	optimista *optimistic*	popular *popular*
arrogante *arrogant*	sociable *sociable*	pesimista *pessimistic*	vulgar *vulgar*
emocionante *exciting*	vulnerable *vulnerable*	feminista *feminist*	ágil *agile*
fascinante *fascinating*	alegre *cheerful*		frágil *fragile*
interesante *interesting*	fuerte *strong*		hábil *skillful*
intrigante *intriguing*			cruel *cruel*

4.3 Write in the blanks the adjectives in the chart that are *not* cognates with English.

_____	_____	_____
pleasant	*nice*	*cheerful*
_____	_____	_____
selfish	*young*	*skillful*

4.4 Write in the blanks the adjectives in the chart that have cognates with more formal English.

_____	_____	_____	_____
proud/arrogant	*friendly/amicable*	*bold/audacious*	*lively/vivacious*

_____

strict/exigent

4.5 Answer these questions.

With what letter do all the adjectives in the first group end? _____

What do all the adjectives in the second group have in common? _____

What do all the adjectives in the third group have in common? _____

Quick Tips

sensible = sensitive   *sensato = sensible*
simpático = nice   *compasivo = sympathetic*
fastidioso = annoying   *melindroso = fastidious*

To Use These Words to Describe People You Know

Look at the following sentences.

¿Cómo es María?   Es inteligente, optimista y joven.
¿Cómo es Carlos?   Es inteligente, optimista y joven.
¿Cómo son María y Carlos?   Son inteligentes, optimistas y jóvenes.

4.6 Now write the patterns.

When an adjective ends in _____ , _____ , or a _____ , it can describe a male or a female.

To describe two or more males or females, add _____ to the adjectives that end in a vowel; add _____ to those that end in a consonant.

Observe the following questions and answers.

¿Es joven Roberto?   — Sí, lo es.   — No, no lo es.

¿Son simpáticos sus hermanos?   — Sí, lo son.   — No, no lo son.

| ¿Es lista Sara? | — Sí, lo es. | — No, no lo es. |
| ¿Son simpáticas sus hermanas? | — Sí, lo son. | — No, no lo son. |

4.7 Fill in the blanks:

To answer a yes-or-no question about a description, you can replace an adjective with _____ , which is placed _____ the verb.

4.8 Use the adjectives in the chart shown above to answer the following questions.

¿Cómo eres?

¿Cómo es una persona en tu familia (tu hermano / tu abuela, etc.)?

¿Cómo son tus amigos?

¿Es idealista tu mejor (*best*) amigo?

4.9 Now write the questions that the following sentences answer.

Es muy interesante.

Son populares.

No, no soy pesimista.

Sí, lo soy.

I Thought You Had to Change the Ending of Adjectives to Show if the Words They Are Describing Are Masculine or Feminine

That is true for the next group—but not for the adjectives we just looked at.

Observe the adjectives in the following chart.

Masculino/Femenino	Masculino/Femenino
activo/activa *active*	conservador/conservadora *conservative*
alto/alta *tall*	encantador/encantadora *charming*
antipático/antipática *disagreeable*	hablador/habladora *talkative*
artístico/artística *artistic*	trabajador/trabajadora *hardworking*

Masculino/Femenino	Masculino/Femenino
bello/bella *lovely*	
bonito/bonita *pretty*	comilón/comilona* *big eater*
bueno/buena *good*	dormilón/dormilona* *big sleeper*
cariñoso/cariñosa *caring, affectionate*	holgazán/holgazana* *lazy*
carismático/carismática *charismatic*	parlanchín/parlanchina* *talkative*
complicado/complicada *complicated*	
creído/creída *conceited, stuck-up*	
delgado/delgada *thin*	
divertido/divertida *fun*	
enérgico/enérgica *energetic*	
flaco/flaca *skinny*	
flojo/floja *lazy*	
franco/franca *frank*	
guapo/guapa *good-looking*	

*When a syllable is added to a word that has a written accent mark on the final syllable, the written accent mark is dropped.

Masculino/Femenino

generoso/generosa
generous

gordo/gorda
plump

hermoso/hermosa
beautiful

lindo/linda
pretty

listo/lista
bright

malo/mala
bad

maravilloso/maravillosa
marvellous

orgulloso/orgullosa
proud

pequeño/pequeña
small

perezoso/perezosa
lazy

perfecto/perfecta
perfect

precioso/preciosa
precious

presumido/presumida
conceited, stuck-up

pulcro/pulcra
neat

Masculino/Femenino

quieto/quieta
quiet

ruidoso/ruidosa
noisy

simpático/simpática
nice

sincero/sincera
honest

tacaño/tacaña
stingy

talentoso/talentosa
talented

terco/terca
stubborn

viejo/vieja
old

vivo/viva
manipulative

4.10 Write the patterns for these adjectives.

When the adjective ends in **o** for a male, it changes to _____ for a female.

When it ends in **-dor** for a male, it ends in _____ for a female.

When the final syllable has an accent mark, and ends in **n** for a male, it adds _____ for a female, and the accent mark _____ .

4.11 Each of the following adjectives matches in *gender* and *number* with one of the nouns below. Write the appropriate one in each blank.

listas   habladora   bueno   pequeños

la mujer _____   los niños _____

las profesoras _____   el médico _____

Don't Forget

All adjectives are plural if the nouns they describe are plural.

Quick Tip

To make the plural of a noun that ends in the letter *z*, change the *z* to *c* and add *es*.

Where are these adjectives positioned in relation to the nouns? Write in any adjective you feel is appropriate for each of the following nouns. Be sure to make it match the noun in gender and number.

la muchacha _____   el chico _____

los hombres _____   las profesoras _____

el abogado _____   la enfermera _____

las actrices _____   el carpintero _____

la madre _____   los jefes _____

el ingeniero _____   las agentes _____

It's a Wrap   Write in your **Vocabulario personal** the adjectives from the above lists that describe yourself or people who are important to you. If the descriptive word you want is not on these lists, look it up in a dictionary, note what category it belongs to, then add it to your list. Add new ones as you need them.

Observe the following sentences.

El señor González es abogado.
Mr. Gonzalez is a lawyer.

El señor González es un abogado bueno.
Mr. Gonzalez is a good lawyer.

María es maestra.
Maria is a teacher.

María es una maestra exigente.
Maria is a strict teacher.

Carlos y Juan son gerentes.
Carlos and Juan are managers.

Carlos y Juan son (unos) gerentes excelentes.
Carlos and Juan are excellent managers.

Ana y Gaby son estudiantes.
Ana and Gaby are students.

Ana y Gaby son (unas) estudiantes listas.
Ana and Gaby are bright students.

4.12   Now write the pattern.

When telling someone's profession, you do not use _____ or _____ .

When giving more information about someone's performance as a member of a profession, use _____ for a man, or _____ for a woman.

4.13 Write the Spanish equivalents for the following:

I'm a student. _____

I'm a responsible student. _____

He's an engineer. _____

He's a capable engineer. _____

She's an accountant. _____

She's a good accountant. _____

They're cooks. _____

They're excellent cooks. _____

Are you a programmer? _____

Is he a specialist? _____

Do Descriptive Adjectives Always Go After the Noun?

Putting a descriptive adjective before the noun generally indicates an inseparable relationship between the two:

El *buen* **esposo** = the husband that we already knew was a good one

El esposo *bueno* = the husband that we are now told is a good one

La *buena* **mujer** = the woman that we already knew was a good one

La mujer *buena* = the woman that we are now told is a good one

El *mal* **hombre** = the man that we already knew was a bad one

El hombre *malo* = the man that we are now told is a bad one

La *mala* mujer = the woman that we already knew was a bad one

La mujer *mala* = the woman that we are now told is a bad one

There is one other adjective—**grande**—that, when placed before the noun, changes in form and meaning. Observe the following:

El *gran* hombre = the great (famous) man

La *gran* mujer = the great (famous) woman

El hombre *grande* = the big (in size) man

La mujer *grande* = the big (in size) woman

4.14 Read the following, then answer the questions.

Ricardo es el hermano de Marta. Es médico. Es un médico muy famoso.

¿Quién es Ricardo?

¿Cuál es su profesión?

¿Cómo es?

Using the above model, describe three of your friends or colleagues. Tell who they are in your life, what they do, and what they are like in their jobs.

To Show Degrees of a Characteristic

Consider the following.

5′11″	6′1″	6′3″
Esteban es alto.	Francisco es <u>bastante</u> alto.	Guillermo es **muy** alto.
5′2″	5′0″	4′10″
Elena es baja.	Sonia es <u>bastante</u> baja.	Ángeles es **muy** baja.

Using adjectives from the charts, describe yourself and two others, using **muy** and **bastante**.

To Compare a Person or People with Others

Observe these sentences.

Esteban es alto, y Francisco <u>también</u>.
Esteban is tall, and so is Francisco.

Sonia es baja, y Ángeles <u>también</u>.
Sonia is short, and so is Angeles.

Esteban <u>no</u> es bajo, ni Francisco <u>tampoco</u>.
Esteban isn't short, and neither is Francisco.

Sonia <u>no</u> es alta, ni Ángeles <u>tampoco</u>.
Sonia isn't tall, and neither is Angeles.

Esteban <u>no</u> es bajo, <u>pero</u> Sonia <u>sí</u>.
Esteban isn't short, but Sonia is.

Esteban es alto, <u>pero</u> Sonia <u>no</u>.
Esteban is tall, but Sonia isn't.

Now describe two of your friends who have the same characteristics.

_____ es _____ , y _____ también.

Describe them with a characteristic that neither has:

_____ no es _____ , ni _____ tampoco.

Now write down a characteristic that one doesn't have but the other does.

_____ no es _____ , pero _____ sí.

Write down a characteristic that one of them has but the other doesn't.

_____ es _____ , pero _____ no.

Do the same four comparisons for two other people.

Observe the following sentences.

Paco es **más alto que** Esteban.
Paco is taller than Esteban.

Esteban es **más bajo que** Paco.
Esteban is shorter than Paco.

Paco **no** es **tan bajo como** Esteban.
Paco isn't as short as Esteban.

Esteban **no** es **tan alto como** Paco.
Esteban isn't as tall as Paco.

4.15 Complete the following.

Elena es **más alta que** Sonia.
Elena is taller than Sonia.

Sonia es _____
Sonia is shorter than Elena.

Elena no es _____ .   Sonia no es _____ .
Elena isn't as short as Sonia.   *Sonia isn't as tall as Elena.*

Now think about four people you know, and compare them with yourself. Follow the model sentences.

María es más independiente que yo.

Carmen no es tan trabajadora como yo.

Pepe es inteligente, y yo también.

Susana no es perezosa, ni yo tampoco.

Observe the following.

Esteban es alto.   Paco es <u>más alto que</u> Esteban.   Guillermo es **el más alto** de todos.
Esteban is tall.   *Paco is taller than Esteban.*   *Guillermo is the tallest of all.*

Elena es baja.   Sonia es <u>más baja que</u> Elena.   Ángeles es **la más baja** de todas.
Elena is short.   *Sonia is shorter than Elena.*   *Angeles is the shortest of all.*

Think about the people you know, and answer the following questions.

¿Quién es la persona más generosa de tu familia?

¿Quién es el actor más talentoso de Hollywood?

¿Quién es la actriz más guapa?

¿Quién es el político más conservador de tu ciudad?

¿Quién es el/la más paciente de tus amigos?

Observe the following.

Sara tiene 2 años.	Gloria tiene 5 años.	Paca tiene 6 años.
Sara is 2 years old.	*Gloria is 5.*	*Paca is 6.*
Sara es menor que Gloria y Paca.	Gloria es mayor que Sara.	Paca es mayor que Sara y Gloria.
Sara is younger than Gloria and Paca.	*Gloria is older than Sara.*	*Paca is older than Sara and Gloria.*
Sara es la menor de las chicas.	Gloria es menor que Paca.	Paca es la mayor de las niñas.
Sara is the youngest of the girls.	*Gloria is younger than Paca.*	*Paca is the eldest of the girls.*

4.16 Now write the equivalents.

older than = _____

the oldest = _____

younger than = _____

the youngest = _____

Observe the following.

Paco tiene 85% en el examen de matemáticas.	Pedro tiene 95% en el examen de matemáticas.	Fernando tiene 100% en el examen de matemáticas.
Paco es bueno en las matemáticas, pero es peor que Pedro y Fernando.	Pedro es mejor que Paco en las matemáticas.	Fernando es mejor que Paco y Pedro en las matemáticas.
Paco es el peor de todos en las matemáticas.	Pedro es peor que Fernando en las matemáticas.	Fernando es el mejor de todos en las matemáticas.

4.17 Now write the equivalents.

better than = _____

the best of all = _____

worse than = _____

the worst of all = _____

It's a Wrap

Practice by talking to yourself out loud and comparing your friends and acquaintances in age and abilities. If your friends understand Spanish, do this exercise in private!

Describing Physical Characteristics

Just as we use the verb *to have* in English to say "He has brown eyes," or "She has curly hair," Spanish uses the verb **tener** to give similar information. Let's look at how **tener** changes to describe different people.

(yo)	tengo *I have*	(nosotros/as)	tenemos *we have*
(tú)	tienes *you have*	(ustedes)	tienen *you all have*
(usted)	tiene *you have*		
(él)	tiene *he has*	(ellos)	tienen *they have*
(ella)	tiene *she has*	(ellas)	tienen *they have*

4.18 Write the pattern.

Start with the **usted/él/ella** form, which ends in the vowel _____ .

To make the **tú** form, add _____ .

To make the **ustedes/ellos/ellas** form, add _____ .

To make the **nosotros** form, start with **tener,** take off the **-er,** and add _____ .

The **yo** form is _____ .

Don't Forget

Only use the subject pronouns—*yo, tú, usted, él, ella, nosotros, nosotras, ustedes, ellos,* and *ellas*—for emphasis or clarification. A good rule is *leave them out* unless someone asks *¿Quién?*

To describe someone's physical characteristics, we need the nouns that refer to different parts of the body (**las partes del cuerpo**).

Observe the following chart.

Masculino		Femenino	
el pelo *hair*	el pecho *chest*	la cabeza *head*	la muñeca *wrist*
el labio *lip*	el estómago *stomach*	la cara *face*	la espalda *back*
el ojo *eye*	el trasero *buttocks*	la ceja *eyebrow*	la cadera *hip*
el diente *tooth*	el muslo *thigh*	la mejilla *cheek*	la pierna *leg*
el cuello *neck*	el tobillo *ankle*	la nariz *nose*	la rodilla *knee*
el dedo *finger*	el talón *heel*	la boca *mouth*	la pantorilla *calf*
el pulgar *thumb*	el pie *foot*	la oreja *ear*	la mano *hand*
el hombro *shoulder*	el dedo del pie *toe*		
el brazo *arm*			

Don't Forget

The parts of the body are nouns—each one has its own gender, which does not change. In other words, a woman has *el pelo, el ojo, el brazo*, just as a man does; a man has *la cabeza, la cara, la pierna*, just as a woman does. The gender belongs to the word—not to the person who has it.

Read, listen to, and learn the next dialogue following the directions given for Dialogue 1.

Dialogue 7   Vecinos Nuevos 🔘

German	Ofelia
Oye, hermana, tenemos vecinos nuevos. Es una familia que tiene dos niños pequeños. *Hey, sis, we have new neighbors. It's a family that has two little children.*	Ay, qué bueno. ¿Cómo son? *Great. What are they like?*
Bueno, el papá es alto, muy flaco y calvo. Tiene barba, pero no tiene bigotes. *Well, the father is tall, really skinny, and bald. He has a beard, but not a mustache.*	Sí, y la mamá, ¿cómo es? *Yes, and the mother—what's she like?*
La mamá es baja, gordita y tiene el pelo negro, largo y rizado. Es bastante guapa. *The mother is short, a little plump, and she has long, black, curly hair. She's really attractive.*	Para ti, hermano, todas las mujeres son guapas. ¿Y los niños? ¿Cómo son? ¿Cuántos años tienen? *According to you, brother, all women are attractive. What are the kids like? How old are they?*
El niño es mayor que la niña. También es más alto. Él tiene 4 años y ella tiene 2. Los dos tienen el pelo negro y los ojos azules. Son preciosos, pero muy tímidos. *The boy is older than the girl. He's also taller. He's 4 and she's 2. Both of them have black hair and blue eyes. They are adorable, but they're really shy.*	Tienes razón. Parece una familia muy atractiva y muy simpática. ¡Tenemos suerte! *You're right. It seems like a very attractive, nice family. We're lucky!*

4.19 Look at the following patterns, then complete the sentences.

The mother has curly hair.   La mamá tiene <u>el pelo rizado</u>.

The mother has black hair.   _____

The mother has long hair.   _____

The father has a curly beard.   El papá tiene <u>la barba rizada</u>.

The father has a black beard.   _____

The father has a long beard.   _____

The boy has blue eyes.   El niño tiene <u>los ojos azules</u>.

The girl has black eyes.   _____

More Adjectives to Describe Hair and Eye Color and Other Features

Some adjectives that describe the parts of the body.

Pelo	Ojos	Otras Partes del Cuerpo
castaño *brown*	azules *blue*	largo/a/os/as *long*
rubio *blond*	color café *brown*	corto/a/os/as *short*
blanco *white*	verdes *green*	grande/s *big*
canoso *gray*	pardos *hazel*	pequeño/a/os/as *little*
negro *black*	negros *black*	fuerte/s *strong*
largo *long*	oscuros *dark*	débil/es *weak*
medio largo *medium length*	claros *light-colored*	musculoso/a/os/as *muscular*
corto *short*	grandes *big*	gordo/a/os/as *fat*
liso, lacio *straight*	pequeños *little*	flaco/a/os/as *skinny*

Pelo	Ojos	Otras Partes del Cuerpo
rizado *curly*	expresivos *expressive*	bonito/a/os/as *pretty*
pintado, teñido *dyed*	bonitos *pretty*	
bonito *pretty*		

Quick Tips

bajo = *short in stature*   corto = *short in length*
grande = *large*   largo = *long*

4.20 Now complete these sentences, following the pattern in the first example.

He has strong legs.   Tiene las piernas fuertes.

She has beautiful eyes.   _____ .

I have long hair.   _____ .

We have hazel eyes.   _____ .

My friend has little feet.   _____ .

He has muscular arms.   _____ .

The girls have curly hair.   _____ .

The men have big shoulders. _____ .

To State Someone's Age

In Spanish, instead of saying how old you *are,* you say how many years you *have.*

¿Cuántos años tiene usted? / ¿Cuánto años tienes?
How old are you?

Tengo nueve años.
I'm nine (years old).

¿Cuántos años tiene Juan?
How old is Juan?

Tiene diez años.
He's ten.

¿Cuántos años tiene Elena?
How old is Elena?

Tiene once años.
She's eleven.

Here are the numbers from 0 to 29, to get started. For higher numbers, look at the chart on p. 82. Or, you could say **Tengo más de veintinueve años**—*I'm over twenty-nine!*

0	1	2	3	4	5	6	7	8	9
cero	uno	dos	tres	cuatro	cinco	seis	siete	ocho	nueve
10	11	12	13	14	15	16	17	18	19
diez	once	doce	trece	catorce	quince	dieciséis	diecisiete	dieciocho	diecinueve
20	21	22	23	24	25	26	27	28	29
veinte	veintiuno	veintidós	veintitrés	veinticuatro	veinticinco	veintiséis	veintisiete	veintiocho	veintinueve

El niño tiene **un** año. La mamá tiene **veintiún** años.
The child is one year old. The mother is twenty-one.

4.21 Practice answering the following questions in complete sentences; then listen to them on the recording, pausing it to answer them again. After you have given your answer, a speaker will give his own personal answer, which will probably not be exactly like yours. Other acceptable answers are given in the Answer Key in the Appendix.

Quick Tip

The "ones"—*uno, veintiuno,* and so on—drop the *o* before a *sustantivo.*

 ¿Cómo eres?

¿Cuántos años tienes?

¿Cómo tiene el pelo tu mejor amigo?

¿Cómo tienen los ojos <u>dos</u> personas de tu familia?

¿Son responsables todos tus amigos?

4.22 Form questions that the following sentences answer.

Sí, tiene el pelo negro también.

No, no es muy generoso.

Cristina y Daniel tienen los ojos azules.

Son bastante simpáticas.

Add to your **Vocabulario personal** the adjectives that describe you and the people important to you. Practice describing your friends and acquaintances out loud—while you are waiting in traffic or doing any other boring activity. It's a great way to make the time useful! Look at the questions at the beginning of this chapter and see if you can now perform all of these activities. **¡Qué bueno!** Good for you!

CHAPTER 5

Identifying and Describing Objects

Do I Need to Read This Chapter?

➜ Can I name the objects that I use every day in my home and my work-place?

➜ Do I know how to ask a Spanish-speaker what something is?

➜ Can I indicate who things belong to?

➜ Can I describe things by size, shape, color, style, and age?

➜ Do I know how to ask people what they have or what they want?

➜ Can I count objects and give quantities?

Get Started

Listen to the following dialogue on the recording. Then play it again, pausing after each sentence in order to repeat it.

Dialogue 8   Los Regalos

Alejandro	Julia
Oye, Julia, ¿qué son estas cosas? *Say, Julia, what are these things?*	Son unos regalos para los niños de mi familia. Ven y te los enseño. *They're a few presents for the children in my family. Come here and I'll show them to you.*
Estas gorras son muy bonitas. ¿Para quiénes son? *These caps are pretty. Who are they for?*	A ver. La gorra blanca es para mi sobrina, Anita. La azul es para Paquito, y la roja, para Sonia. *Let's see. The white cap is for my niece, Anita. The blue one is for Paquito, and the red one is for Sonia.*
¿Y estos guantes? *And these gloves?*	Ésos son para los mismos niños, pues hacen juego con las gorras. *They're for the same children—they match the caps.*
Bien. ¿Para quiénes son los juguetes? *OK, who are the toys for?*	Bueno, hay un juguete pequeño para cada niño. *Well, there's a small toy for each child.*
¡Pero si ya tienen cantidad de juguetes! *But they already have loads of toys!*	No importa. Mira, estos cochecitos son para Paquito y las muñecas son para las niñas. *That doesn't matter. Look, these little cars are for Paquito, and the dolls are for the girls.*
Hay otra caja en el rincón. ¿Qué es eso? *There's another box in the corner. What's that?*	Mi amor, lo que está en esa caja es un regalo para ti, y es un secreto. *Sweetheart, what's in that box is a present for you—and it's a secret.*

To Find Out What Things Are Called in Spanish

Observe the following questions and answers.

¿Qué es esto? (*ke <u>ses</u> to*)
What's this?

Es un libro.
It's a book.

Es una revista.
It's a magazine.

¿Qué es eso? (*ke <u>se</u> so*)
What's that?

Es un libro.
It's a book.

Es una revista.
It's a magazine.

¿Qué son estas cosas?
What are these (things)?

Son (unos) libros.
They're books.

Son (unas) revistas
They're magazines.

¿Qué son esas cosas?
What are those (things)?

Son (unos) libros.
They're books.

Son (unas) revistas.
They're magazines.

Quick Tips

esto = *this*
estos = *these*

eso = *that*
esos = *those*

If you can touch it, use *esto* (with a *t*).
If you can't touch it, use *eso*.

Following are several items that may be important to you in your daily life. Go down the list asking yourself **¿Qué es esto?** if you have the item nearby, or **¿Qué es eso?** if it is beyond your reach.

Masculino	**Femenino**
el periódico *newspaper*	la taza de café/te *cup of coffee/tea*
el libro *book*	la comida *meal, food*
el bolígrafo *ballpoint pen*	la tarjeta de crédito *credit card*
el papel *piece of paper*	la mesa *table*
el teléfono *telephone*	la silla *chair*
el coche / el carro / el automóvil *car*	la casa *house*
el refresco *cold drink*	la computadora *computer*

Now write the plural of each of the following nouns, and ask yourself **¿Qué son estas cosas?** or **¿Qué son esas cosas?** Don't forget to include **los** or **las**.

_____	_____	_____
newspapers	*chairs*	*computers*
_____	_____	_____
credit cards	*tables*	*houses*
_____	_____	_____
pieces of paper	*meals*	*cups of coffee*
_____	_____	_____
ballpoint pens	*telephones*	*cold drinks*
_____	_____	
books	*cars*	

Quick Tips

la carta = letter   *la tarjeta = card*

To Learn the Names of Things

First, think about the objects that you see or use every day—the things you are likely to talk about. Following are some nouns listed according to the places they are likely to be found. Go through the lists and decide which ones are relevant for you, then add them to your personal vocabulary list.

Nouns for the *Classroom* (*el aula / el salón de clase*)

Masculino		Femenino	
el lápiz *pencil*	el papel *paper*	la pluma *pen*	la silla *chair*
el bolígrafo *ballpoint pen*	el cuaderno *notebook*	la pizarra *blackboard*	la mesa *table*
el escritorio *teacher's desk*	el mapa *map*	la tiza *chalk*	la puerta *door*
el pupitre *student desk*	el reloj *clock*	la pared *wall*	la ventana *window*
		la lámpara *light*	la lección *lesson*

Nouns for the *Office* (*la oficina* / *el despacho*)

Masculino	Femenino
el fax *fax machine / fax message*	la oficina *office*
el teléfono *telephone*	la computadora *computer*
el celular *cell phone*	la computadora portátil *laptop*
el calendario *calendar*	la impresora *printer*
el archivo *file*	la calculadora *calculator*
el folleto *brochure*	la fotocopiadora *copier*
el diccionario *dictionary*	la estantería *bookcase*
el mensaje de correo electrónico *email message*	la agenda *diary*
	la carta *letter*
	la nota *memo*
	la carpeta *folder*

Nouns for the *House*

Masculino	Femenino
el comedor *dining room*	la casa *house*
el baño *bathroom*	la sala *living room*

Masculino	Femenino
el dormitorio / el cuarto *bedroom*	la televisión *television program*
el sillón *easy chair*	la radio *radio program*
el sofá *sofa*	la cocina *kitchen*
el televisor *television set*	la cortina *curtain*
el video *VCR, videotape*	la alfombra *rug*
el lector de discos compactos *CD player*	la estufa *stove*
el radio *radio*	la refrigeradora *refrigerator*
el cuadro *picture*	la cama *bed*
el horno *oven*	la tina *bathtub*
el microondas *microwave oven*	la ducha *shower*
el fregadero *kitchen sink*	la lámpara *light fixture, lamp*
el lavaplatos *dishwasher*	la luz *daylight, electricity*
el lavabo *bathroom sink*	la calefacción *heating*
el inodoro *toilet*	el agua* *water*
el apartamento *apartment*	
el aire acondicionado *air-conditioning*	

*__el agua__ is really feminine, but uses __el__ for pronunciation purposes. Its adjectives are feminine: __el agua fría__ = *cold water*.

Nouns for *Outdoors*

Masculino	Femenino
el perro *dog (male)*	la perra *dog (female)*
el gato *cat (male)*	la gata *cat (female)*
el jardín *garden, yard*	la bicicleta *bicycle*
el coche / el carro *car*	la motocicleta *motorcycle*
el garaje *garage*	la flor *flower*
el árbol *tree*	
el sendero *path*	

What's Missing from These Lists? What Objects Are Important to You?

Find in your dictionary the names of things you need that are not listed here, then add them to your **Vocabulario personal.** Be sure to include the **el** or **la,** and practice writing out the plurals. You might want to write the words on small pieces of paper and stick them on objects in your home and office.

Look at the following.

¿Qué es esto? *What's this?*	Es un regalo. *It's a present.*	¿Qué es esto? *What is this?*	Es un suéter. *It's a sweater.*
¿De quién es? *Who is it from?*	Es de mi hermana. *It's from my sister.*	¿De quién es? *Whose is it?*	Es de Ana. *It's Ana's.*
			Es su suéter nuevo. *It's her new sweater.*

◇
**Test
Yourself**

5.1 Fill in the blanks.

The two meanings of **¿De quién es?** are _____ and _____ .

5.2 Write the equivalents.

_____	_____
What's this?	*It's a book.*
_____	_____
Whose is it?	*It's Juan's.*
_____	_____
What's that?	*It's a credit card.*
_____	_____
Whose is it?	*It's Sra. Diaz's.*
_____	_____
What are these?	*They're cars.*
_____	_____
Whose are they?	*They're Ana's and Raul's.*
_____	_____
What are those?	*They're bicycles.*
_____	_____
Whose are they?	*They're Carlos's and Pedro's.*
_____	Es un anillo de compromiso.
What's this?	*It's an engagement ring.*
_____	_____
Whose is it?	*It's Jimena's.*
_____	_____
Who is it from?	*It's from Jimena's boyfriend.*

What Are the Adjectives That Describe Things?

Look at the following questions and answers.

¿Cómo es?   ¿Cómo son?
What is it like?   *What are they like?*

¿De qué tamaño es?   ¿De qué tamaño son?
What size is it? / How big is it?   *What size are they? / How big are they?*

Adjectives That Describe Sizes

pequeño/a/os/as *small*	mediano/a/os/as *medium*	grande(s) *large*
chico/a/os/as *small*	normal(es) *average*	enorme(s) *huge*
largo/a/os/as *long*	medio largo *medium*	corto/a/os/as *short*
ancho/a/os/as *wide*	angosto/a/os/as *narrow*	

¿De qué forma es?   ¿De qué forma son?
What shape is it?   *What shape are they?*

Here are some adjectives that describe shapes:

redondo/a/os/as	cuadrado/a/os/as	rectangular(es)	triangular(es)	rómbico/a/os/as
round	*square*	*rectangular*	*triangular*	*diamond-shaped*

¿De qué color es?   ¿De qué color son?
What color is it?   *What color are they?*

Adjectives That Describe Colors

Using colored markers, fill in each circle with the appropriate color.

○	○	○	○
rojo/a/os/as *red*	amarillo/a/os/as *yellow*	azul(es) *blue*	verde(s) *green*
○	○	○	○
morado/a/os/as *purple*	anaranjado/a/os/as *orange*	blanco/a/os/as *white*	negro/a/os/as *black*
○	○	○	
gris(es) *gray*	marrón/marrones *brown*	de muchos colores *multicolored*	

Observe the following sentences.

La caja es triangular, pequeña y roja.

El cuadro es cuadrado, grande y de muchos colores.

Las pelotas son redondas y azules.

Los paquetes son blancos, medio grandes y rectangulares.

5.3 Now answer the questions.

¿De qué color es la caja?

¿De qué tamaño es el cuadro?

¿De qué forma son las pelotas?

¿De qué color y tamaño son los paquetes?

Here are some adjectives that describe other qualities. The words listed after a slash are **sinónimos**—they have similar meaning. The **antónimos** in the right column have the opposite meaning of the words in the left column.

interesante(s) *interesting*	aburrido/a/os/as *boring*
caro/a/os/as *expensive*	barato/a/os/as *cheap*
complicado/a/os/as, difícil(es) *complicated, difficult*	sencillo/a/os/as, fácil(es) *simple, easy*
correcto/a/os/as *correct*	incorrecto/a/os/as *incorrect*
moderno/a/os/as *modern*	anticuado/a/os/as *old-fashioned*
nuevo/a/os/as *new*	viejo/a/os/as, antiguo/a/os/as *old, very old*
pesado/a/os/as *heavy*	ligero/a/os/as *lightweight*
elegante(s) *fancy/elegant*	ordinario/a/os/as *plain*
raro/a/os/as *strange/rare*	común/comunes, corriente(s) *common, ordinary*

Quick Tip

To emphasize that something is extraordinary, spell SOCKS in English (keeping your vowels frozen).

S – O – C – K – S

eso sí que es	malo,	bueno,	maravilloso,	imposible,	etcétera
That certainly is	*bad*	*good*	*wonderful*	*impossible,*	*and so on.*

To say "No way!" just say S-O-C-K-no

¡Eso sí que no!

Objects can also be described by the material from which they are made. The materials are nouns.

¿De qué material es?   Es de madera.
What is it made of?   *It's made of wood.*

Common Materials

de tela	de madera	de metal	de piedra
of fabric	*of wood*	*of metal*	*of stone*
de seda	de plástico	de hierro	de diamantes
of silk	*of plastic*	*of iron*	*of diamonds*
de lana	de cuero	de cobre	de rubíes
of wool	*of leather*	*of copper*	*of rubies*
de algodón	de vidrio	de plata	de perlas
of cotton	*of glass*	*of silver*	*of pearls*
de tela sintética	de papel	de oro	
of synthetic fabric	*of paper*	*of gold*	

Objects can be described by the category they belong to. Following are some typical questions and answers.

¿De qué tipo es el coche?   Es un convertible.
What kind of car is it? / What kind is it?   *It's a convertible.*

¿De qué marca es el coche?   Es un *Jaguar*.
What make is the car?   *It's a Jaguar.*

Look around you and determine five familiar objects. For each one, ask and answer aloud in Spanish the following questions.

What is it?   *Whose is it?*   *What is it like?*
What size, shape, color, type, and make is it?

Telling What People Have and What They Want

Learn the following dialogue by following the usual steps.

Dialogue 9   *En una tienda de ropa.*

Buenos días, señorita. Mi hija no tiene su uniforme para la escuela. ¿Tienen ustedes los uniformes para el colegio Santa Ana?
Good morning. My daughter doesn't have her school uniform. Do you have uniforms for St. Ann's?

Sí, señora, los tenemos para todas las escuelas de la ciudad. ¿De qué talla es su hija?
Yes, we have them for all the schools in the city. What size is your daughter?

Ella quiere una blusa y una falda de talla 6, y la chaqueta de talla 8.
She wants a blouse and skirt in size 6 and the jacket in size 8.

Muy bien, a ver. . . sí, tengo aquí la blusa y la falda y la chaqueta de talla 6, pero la chaqueta de talla 8, no tengo.
OK, let's see . . . yes, I have here the blouse, skirt, and jacket in size 6, but I don't have the jacket in size 8.

Entonces, queremos la blusa y la falda. ¿Cuánto es?
Then we want the blouse and skirt. How much are they?

Son cincuenta dólares.
They're $50.

Bueno, aquí tiene usted los 50 dólares. ¿En qué tienda tienen las chaquetas más grandes?
OK, here's the $50. What store has bigger jackets?

Gracias, señora. Las tienen en la tienda Estrella, aquí enfrente. A propósito, ¿quiere su hija los zapatos?
Thank you, ma'am. They have them in the store called Estrella across the street. By the way, does your daughter want shoes?

Masculino	Femenino
el traje *suit*	la camiseta *T-shirt*
el saco *suit jacket*	la blusa *blouse*
el sombrero *hat*	la corbata *necktie*
el cinturón *belt*	la bufanda *scarf*
el conjunto *outfit*	la falda *skirt*
el suéter *sweater*	las medias *stockings*
el pijama *pajamas*	la ropa interior *underwear*
los calcetines *socks*	la bata *robe*
los zapatos *shoes*	las pantuflas *slippers*
los pantalones *pants*	la chaqueta *jacket*
el abrigo *overcoat*	
los guantes *gloves*	

Make a list of ten items of clothing (**prendas de vestir**) that you have in your closet, and scribe them. Follow the example sentence.

Tengo una camisa blanca de algodón.

Now write five sentences describing clothing you want.

Find in the dictionary the names of other articles of clothing that you have or wa'
Describe them aloud, then add them to your **Vocabulario personal.**

No, gracias, no queremos más.
Muchísimas gracias. Hasta luego.
No, thank you. We don't want anything else.
Thanks very much. Bye.

Hasta luego, señora.
Good-bye, ma'am.

To talk about what people *have* or what they *want,* we need to look at two important verbs: **tener** and **querer.**

We used **tener** earlier to describe the parts of the body. We can use the same forms to tell what *things* we have. Compare these forms with those of **querer.**

Observe the following.

	tener	querer
(yo)	tengo *I have*	quiero *I want*
(tú)	tienes *you have*	quieres *you want*
(Ud.*/él/ella)	tiene *you have* *he has* *she has*	quiere *you want* *he wants* *she wants*
(Uds.†/ellos/ellas)	tienen *you all have* *they have*	quieren *you all want* *they want*
(nosotros/nosotras)	tenemos *we have*	queremos *we want*

*Ud. = usted

†Uds. = ustedes

5.4 Now write the patterns.

-o at the end of a verb means **yo.**

-s at the end of a verb means _____ .

-e at the end of a verb means _____ , _____ , or _____ .

-n at the end of a verb means _____ , _____ , or _____ .

-mos at the end of a verb means _____ or _____ .

Don't Forget

Use the subject pronouns (*yo, tú, él, ella*, etc.) only when you want to emphasize the person who has or wants something. For example:

Él tiene el libro, (pero ella no).
He has the book, (but she doesn't.)

Ella quiere los zapatos, (pero yo no).
She wants the shoes, (but I don't.)

5.5 Practice answering the following questions in complete sentences; then listen to them on the recording, pausing it to answer them again. After you have given your answer, a speaker will give his own personal answer, which will probably not be exactly like yours. Other acceptable answers are given in the Answer Key in the Appendix.

¿Qué tienes en tu casa?

¿Qué quieres en tu casa?

¿Qué tiene tu amigo en su oficina?

¿Qué quiere tu amigo en su oficina?

En la casa de tu familia, ¿tienen ustedes una computadora?

¿Quieren ustedes una computadora nueva?

¿Tienen ustedes vecinos?

¿Tienen sus vecinos un coche?

5.6 Now write questions that the following statements answer.

No, no tengo un coche grande.

Sí, tengo una casa bonita.

Mi amiga tiene una tarjeta de crédito.

No, mis amigos no tienen apartamento.

Tenemos una oficina nueva.

Ella tiene unos zapatos negros, pero yo no.

Observe the following sentences.

¿Tienes el libro?   Sí, lo tengo. / No, n
Do you have the book?   *Yes, I have it. / No, I d*

¿Tienes los libros?   Sí, los tengo. / No,
Do you have the books?   *Yes, I have them. / No,*

¿Tienes la revista?   Sí, la tengo. / No, n
Do you have the magazine?   *Yes, I have it. / No, I d*

¿Tienes las revistas?   Sí, las tengo. / No,
Do you have the magazines?   *Yes, I have them. / No,*

5.7 Write the patterns.

To say the equivalent of the object *it* for a ma

To say the equivalent of the object *it* for a fen

To say the equivalent of the object *them* for a

To say the equivalent of the object *them* for a

The equivalents of the objects *it* and *them* are

5.8 Now complete the following.

¿Quieres las fotografías?   _____
                                 Yes, I want the

¿Quieres el coche?   _____
                          No, I don't wa

¿Quieres la computadora?   _____
                                No, I don't wa

¿Quieres los bolígrafos?   _____
                                No, I don't wa

Here is a list of nouns that represent articles of cloth noun belongs to the *word,* not to the person who has it

Masculino	Femer
el vestido	la cam
dress	*shirt*

It's a W

Nouns That Represent Positive Aspects of Life

Masculino	Femenino
el amor *love*	la bondad *goodness*
el dinero *money*	la felicidad *happiness*
el éxito *success*	la tranquilidad *calm*
el interés *interest*	la seguridad *security*
el trabajo *work*	la amistad *friendship*
el perdón *forgiveness*	la responsabilidad *responsibility*
el conocimiento *knowledge*	la comprensión *understanding*
el reconocimiento *recognition*	la pasión *passion*
el agradecimiento *appreciation*	la emoción *excitement*
	la perfección *perfection*
	la satisfacción *satisfaction*
	la sabiduría *wisdom*
	la energía *energy*
	la fuerza *power*
	la riqueza *wealth*

Masculino	Femenino
	la belleza *beauty*
	la confianza *confidence*
	la salud *health*
	la virtud *virtue*
	la gratitud *appreciation*
	la paz *peace*
	la suerte *luck*

Quick Tip

When Spanish-speakers make a toast, they wish each other *"salud, dinero y amor."*

5.9 Sometimes (but not always) we can tell what gender a noun belongs to by its ending. Looking at the preceding list, find the answers to the following.

The endings _____ , _____ , _____ , and _____ indicate a feminine noun.

The ending _____ indicates a masculine noun.

Nouns That Represent Negative Aspects of Life

Masculino	Femenino
el odio *hatred*	la guerra *war*
el fracaso *failure*	la desdicha *unhappiness*
el rencor *resentment/grudge*	la indiferencia *indifference*

Masculino	Femenino
	la ignorancia *ignorance*
	la pobreza *poverty*
	la estupidez *stupidity*
	la tensión *stress*
	la incomprensión *lack of understanding*
	la enemistad *enmity*
	la inseguridad *insecurity*
	la fealdad *ugliness*
	la maldad *evil*
	la irresponsabilidad *irresponsibility*
	la enfermedad *sickness*
	el hambre* *hunger*

***el hambre** is like **el agua**: it is really feminine, but it uses **el** just for pronunciation purposes. Its adjectives are feminine.

5.10 Complete the following chart by filling in the **antónimos**—words with opposite meanings. Be sure to include the **el** or **la**.

Aspectos Positivos	Aspectos Negativos
la seguridad	la inseguridad
_____	la maldad
el éxito	_____
_____	la enfermedad
la belleza	_____
_____	el odio
la riqueza	_____
_____	la ignorancia
el interés	_____
_____	la tensión

5.11 Answer the following questions, following the pattern of the example.

Pregunta (*Question*)	Respuesta (*Answer*)
¿Tienes tensión en tu vida?	Sí, la tengo. / No, no la tengo.
¿Quieres éxito?	_____ .
¿Tienen tus amigos trabajo?	_____ .
¿Quién tiene sabiduría?	_____ .
¿Quieren reconocimiento tú y tus amigos?	_____ .

5.12 Now write questions for the answers below.

Pregunta	Respuesta
_____ .	Sí, lo tengo.
_____ .	No, no la quiere.
_____ .	Sí, lo queremos.
_____ .	No, no la tienen.
_____ .	Mi mejor amigo lo tiene, pero yo no.

Saying That Something Exists

Spanish has one easy word to indicate that things exist: **hay**. For example:

Hay un libro en la mesa.
There is a book on the table.

Hay cuatro libros en la mesa.
There are four books on the table.

Hay dinero en el banco.
There is money in the bank.

Hay felicidad en todas partes.
There is happiness everywhere.

Learn the next dialogue by following the usual steps.

Diálogo 10   *Un maestro y la directora de la escuela.* ◉

Guillermo, el Maestro de Español	Elena, la Directora de la Escuela
Oye, Elena, ¿cuántas clases del primer nivel hay en la próxima sesión? *Say, Elena, how many first-level classes are there in the upcoming session?*	Mira, Guillermo, hay cinco clases del primer nivel. *Look, Guillermo, there are five level 1 classes.*

Guillermo, el Maestro de Español	Elena, la Directora de la Escuela
¿Y cuántas tengo yo? *And how many do I have?*	Tú tienes tres. *You have three.*
Ay, ¡qué bueno! ¿Cuántos estudiantes hay en cada clase? *Great! How many students are there in each class?*	Fíjate que hay treinta y dos estudiantes en cada grupo. *But take note that there are thirty-two students in each group.*
¡Treinta y dos! ¡Qué malo está eso! *Thirty-two! That's really bad.*	Sí. Las clases son demasiado grandes. *Yes. The classes are too big.*
Esto no es bueno ni para los maestros ni para los estudiantes. *This isn't good for the teachers or the students.*	Tienes razón. Es un problema muy grande para todos. *You're right. It's a big problem for everybody.*

5.13 Answer the following questions.

¿Quién es Guillermo?

¿Cuál es el nombre de la directora?

¿Cuántas clases del primer nivel hay?

¿Cuántos estudiantes hay en cada grupo?

To Ask and Say How Many There Are of Something

Look at these examples.

¿Cuántos médicos hay en el grupo? *How many doctors are there in the group?*	Hay cuatro. *There are four.*
¿Cuántos hijos tienes? *How many children do you have?*	Tengo tres hijos. *I have three.*
¿Cuántos periódicos quieres? *How many newspapers do you want?*	Quiero un periódico. *I want one newspaper.*
¿Cuántas hijas tienes? *How many daughters do you have?*	Tengo una hija. *I have one daughter.*
¿Cuántas camisas quiere la señora? *How many shirts does the lady want?*	Quiere dos camisas. *She wants two shirts.*
¿Cuántas niñas hay en el club? *How many girls are there in the club?*	Hay nueve. *There are nine.*

5.14 Fill in the blanks.

To ask *how many,* use _____ when the items you are counting are masculine.

When the items you are counting are feminine, use _____ .

Is *How Much* Different from *How Many*?

Yes. To say *how much,* use **¿Cuánto?** or **¿Cuánta?**

¿Cuánto dinero tienes?
How much money do you have?

Tengo muy poco.
I have very little.

¿Cuánto tiempo tenemos?
How much time do we have?

Tenemos dos horas.
We have two hours.

¿Cuánta responsabilidad tiene?
How much responsibility does he have?

Tiene mucha.
He has a lot.

To Say There Is Something—or Nothing

Observe the following.

Hay algo en el coche.
There is something in the car.

No hay nada en el coche.
There is nothing in the car.

Hay alguien en la sala.
There is somebody in the living room.

No hay nadie en la sala.
There's nobody in the living room.

5.15 Write the equivalents and fill in the blank.

something = _____   somebody = _____

nothing = _____   nobody = _____

When you use a negative word, put _____ before the verb.

It's a Wrap

Look around you and indicate what you see nearby. Ask how much there is or how many there are of each item, and answer each question.

Numbers from 30 Up

30	31	32	33	34	35	36	37	38	39
treinta	treinta y uno	treinta y dos	treinta y tres	treinta y cuatro	treinta y cinco	treinta y seis	treinta y siete	treinta y ocho	treinta y nueve
40	41	42	43	44	45	46	47	48	49
cuarenta	cuarenta y uno	cuarenta y dos	cuarenta y tres	cuarenta y cuatro	cuarenta y cinco	cuarenta y seis	cuarenta y siete	cuarenta y ocho	cuarenta y nueve
50	51	52	53	54	55	56	57	58	59
cincuenta	cincuenta y uno	cincuenta y dos	cincuenta y tres	cincuenta y cuatro	cincuenta y cinco	cincuenta y seis	cincuenta y siete	cincuenta y ocho	cincuenta y nueve
60	61	62	63	64	65	66	67	68	69
sesenta	sesenta y uno	sesenta y dos	sesenta y tres	sesenta y cuatro	sesenta y cinco	sesenta y seis	sesenta y siete	sesenta y ocho	sesenta y nueve
70	71	72	73	74	75	76	77	78	79
setenta	setenta y uno	setenta y dos	setenta y tres	setenta y cuatro	setenta y cinco	setenta y seis	setenta y siete	setenta y ocho	setenta y nueve
80	81	82	83	84	85	86	87	88	89
ochenta	ochenta y uno	ochenta y dos	ochenta y tres	ochenta y cuatro	ochenta y cinco	ochenta y seis	ochenta y siete	ochenta y ocho	ochenta y nueve
90	91	92	93	94	95	96	97	98	99
noventa	noventa y uno	noventa y dos	noventa y tres	noventa y cuatro	noventa y cinco	noventa y seis	noventa y siete	noventa y ocho	noventa y nueve

100	101	102	113	154	165	176	188	197
cien	**ciento uno**	ciento dos	ciento trece	ciento cincuenta y cuatro	ciento sesenta y cinco	ciento setenta y seis	ciento ochenta y ocho	ciento noventa y siete

200	201	202	212	256	293
doscientos	doscientos uno	doscientos dos	doscientos doce	doscientos cincuenta y seis	doscientos noventa y tres

300	400	500	600	700	800	900
trescientos	**cuatrocientos**	**quinientos**	**seiscientos**	**setecientos**	**ochocientos**	**novecientos**

1000	1492	1776	1999	2000	2003
mil	mil cuatrocientos noventa y dos	mil setecientos setenta y seis	mil novecientos noventa y nueve	dos mil	dos mil tres

1.000.000	2.472.683
un millón	**dos millones, cuatrocientos setenta y dos mil, seiscientos ochenta y tres**

A good way to practice numbers is by getting all your friends' addresses and telephone numbers and saying them aloud. Use the following formulas.

¿Cuál es tu dirección?
What's your address?

Mi dirección es: C/ Bolívar 21   28014 Madrid

(Calle Bolívar veintiuno   veintiocho catorce Madrid)

¿Cuál es tu número de teléfono?
What's your telephone number?

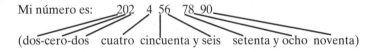

Mi número es: 202   4 56   78 90

(dos-cero-dos   cuatro cincuenta y seis   setenta y ocho noventa)

Quick Tip

In English, we often put the word *and* after the hundreds, as in "a hundred *and* thirty-nine."

In Spanish, the *and* never goes after the hundreds, but always goes with the tens, as in 139: *ciento treinta y nueve.*

In English, a comma is used to indicate thousands, and a period is used as a decimal point. In Spanish, it is just the opposite.

English	*Spanish*
4,562.50	4.562,50
4,578,320.75	4.578.320,75

5.16 Write the following numbers in words.

_____　　　_____　　　_____
3　　　　　　　　　64　　　　　　　　72

_____　　　_____
31　　　　　　　　546

_____
7.892

Can you perform all of the tasks mentioned at the beginning of the chapter? **¿Sí? ¡Eso sí que es fantástico!**

◆◆◆

CHAPTER 6

Telling Times and Dates

◆◆◆

Do I Need to Read This Chapter?

➡ Can I ask or tell someone what time it is?

➡ Can I give today's day and date in Spanish?

➡ Do I know the words for the events in my life—and how to tell when and where they will take place?

To Tell the Time in Spanish

To tell the time, you need **un reloj**:

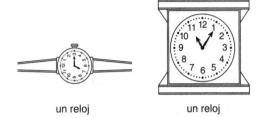

un reloj   un reloj

To ask what time it is, say:

¿Qué hora es?   (*ke o ra es*)

Test Yourself

6.1 Look at the following **relojes,** and continue the exercise, following the first examples.

Es la una.   Son las dos.   Son las tres.   Son las cuatro.

_____   _____   _____   _____

_____   _____   _____   _____

If it is 12 o'clock, you can say:

Es mediodía.   or   Es medianoche.
It's twelve noon.   *It's twelve midnight.*

To Express *a.m.* and *p.m.*

If it is between midnight and sunrise, say **de la madrugada**.

> Son las cuatro de la madrugada.
> *It's four a.m.*

If it is between sunrise and lunchtime, say **de la mañana**.

> Son las diez de la mañana.
> *It's ten a.m.*

If it is between lunchtime and nightfall, say **de la tarde**.

> Son las tres de la tarde.
> *It's three p.m.*

If it is between nightfall and midnight, say **de la noche**.

> Son las once de la noche.
> *It's eleven p.m.*

What About the In-Between Times?

To tell the minutes after the hour, add **y** plus the number of minutes.

> Son las seis y cinco.
> *It's five after six.*

> Son las seis y quince. / Son las seis y cuarto.
> *It's six-fifteen. / It's a quarter after six.*

To tell the minutes before the hour, add **menos** plus the number of minutes.

> Son las siete menos diez.
> *It's ten to seven.*

> Son las nueve menos quince. / Son las nueve menos cuarto.
> *It's fifteen to nine. / It's a quarter to nine.*

To tell the half hour, add **y media**.

> Es la una y media.
> *It's one-thirty.*

Don't Forget

Only one o'clock uses *es;*
all other hours are *son.*

Son las dos y media.
It's two-thirty.

6.2 Write the equivalents.

_____ .   _____ .

It's 3:15 a.m.   *It's 4:30 p.m.*

_____ .   _____ .

It's 7:05 a.m.   *It's 10:40 p.m.*

Names of the Days of the Week

Look at the calendar days below, then observe the sentences that follow.

lunes	martes	miércoles	jueves	viernes	sábado	domingo

Hay siete días en una semana.
There are seven days in a week.

El primer día de la semana es lunes.
The first day of the week is Monday.

El día después del lunes es martes.
The day after Monday is Tuesday.

El día antes del jueves es miércoles.
The day before Thursday is Wednesday.

El sábado y el domingo son el fin de semana.
Saturday and Sunday are the weekend.

¿Qué día es hoy?
What day is today?

6.3 Fill in the blanks.

The week begins with _____ instead of Sunday.

The names of the days are spelled with a _____ letter.

_____ means "after."

_____ means "before."

_____ means " today."

6.4 Answer the following questions.

¿Cuál es el primer día de la semana?

¿Qué día es antes del domingo?

¿Qué día es después del viernes?

¿Cuántos días hay en una semana?

¿Qué día es hoy?

6.5 Write a question for each of the following answers.

Es miércoles.

Hay siete.

Son los días del fin de semana.

Es jueves.

Es lunes.

To Tell the Date

Study the names of the months.

enero	abril	julio	octubre
febrero	mayo	agosto	noviembre
marzo	junio	septiembre	diciembre

6.6 Now fill in the blanks.

El primer mes es enero.

El mes después de enero es _____ .

El mes antes de mayo es _____ .

El mes antes de diciembre es _____ .

El mes después de diciembre es _____ .

Hay _____ meses en un año.

Observe the following sentences.

¿Qué fecha es? / ¿Cuál es la fecha?
What's the date?

Es el primero de marzo.   Es el dos de octubre.
It's March the first.   *It's October the second.*

Es el ocho de mayo.   Es el trece de agosto.
It's May the eighth.   *It's August the thirteenth.*

6.7 Fill in the blanks.

The months are written in Spanish with a _____ letter.

In English, ordinal numbers—like *second, fourth, fifteenth*—are used with dates.

In Spanish, cardinal numbers—like **dos, cuatro, quince**—are used with dates, with one exception: _____ indicates "the first."

6.8 Express the following in Spanish.

_____   _____

It's June the twentieth.   *It's October the sixth.*

_____   _____

It's May the thirtieth.   *It's April the eighteenth.*

More dates

El Año Nuevo es el primero de enero.
New Year's Day is the first of January.

El Día de Independencia de los Estados Unidos es el cuatro de julio.
Independence Day in the United States is the fourth of July.

El Día del Trabajo es el primer lunes de septiembre en los Estados Unidos.
Labor Day is the first Monday in September in the United States.

El Día del Trabajo es el primero de mayo en otros países.
Labor Day is the first of May in other countries.

El Día de los Enamorados es el catorce de febrero.
Valentine's Day is the fourteenth of February.

El Día de los Inocentes es el primero de abril en los Estados Unidos.
April Fool's Day is the first of April in the United States.

El Día de los Inocentes es el veintiocho de diciembre en los países hispanos.
The "Day to Trick the Unaware" is the twenty-eighth of December in Hispanic countries.

El veintitrés de noviembre es el cumpleaños de mi hijo.
November the twenty-third is my son's birthday.

Answer the following.

¿Cuál es la fecha de tu cumpleaños?

¿Qué otras fechas son importantes para ti?

Observe the following.

el primero / la primera	el tercero / la tercera
the first / the first one	*the third / the third one*
el primer día	el tercer día
the first day	*the third day*
el primer lunes	el tercer lunes
the first Monday	*the third Monday*
la primera semana	la tercera semana
the first week	*the third week*

6.9 Now write the patterns.

"the first" before a masculine noun = _____

"the third" before a masculine noun = _____

"the first" before a feminine noun = _____

"the third" before a feminine noun = _____

"the first one," when referring to a masculine noun = _____

"the first one," when referring to a feminine noun = _____

6.10 Write the equivalents.

_____   _____
the first year   *the third house*

_____   _____
the first hour   *the third building*

_____   _____
the first one (a street)   *the third one (a traffic light)*

Quick Tip

When abbreviating the date, put the day first, then the month, then the year. For example: 2/10/04 = *el dos de octubre del 2004.*

Telling About Events

Una invitación informal

FIESTA

este viernes

el 10 de marzo

a las ocho de la tarde

en la casa de Luisa

para celebrar el cumpleaños de Silvia

Learn the following dialogue, following the usual steps.

Dialogue 11   Una fiesta.

Sara	Benjamín
¿Qué es eso? *What's that?*	Mira, es una invitación a una fiesta. *Look, it's an invitation to a party.*
¿Ah, sí? ¿Cuándo es? *Really? When is it?*	Es el próximo viernes. *It's next Friday.*
¿Dónde es —y a qué hora? *Where is it—and at what time?*	Pues, es en la casa de Luisa, a las ocho. *Um, it's at Luisa's, at eight o'clock.*
¡Qué bueno! ¿Cuál es el motivo? *Great! What's the occasion?*	Es el cumpleaños de Silvia. *It's Silvia's birthday.*
¿La fiesta es una sorpresa? *Is the party a surprise?*	La verdad, no sé. *I really don't know.*

A **fiesta** is an example of a noun that indicates **un acontecimiento**—an event. Let's look at some other nouns that name **acontecimientos importantes**.

Masculino	Femenino
el concierto *concert*	la fiesta *party*
el partido *game*	la película *movie*
el campeonato *championship game*	la reunión *meeting*
el concurso *contest*	la junta *meeting*
el debate *debate*	la charla *chat*
el discurso *speech/lecture*	la tertulia *social-cultural event*
el festival *festival*	la clase *class*
el espectáculo *show*	la feria *fair*
el programa *program*	la pieza de teatro *play*
el drama *drama*	la comedia *comedy*
el funeral *funeral*	la boda *wedding*
el servicio *service*	la cena *dinner*
el desayuno *breakfast*	la comida *main meal of the day*
el almuerzo *lunch*	la merienda *afternoon tea*
el recital *recital*	la conferencia *lecture/talk*
el ensayo *rehearsal*	la exposición *exhibit*

Masculine	Feminine
el compromiso *commitment*	la cita (con el médico, el dentista, etc.) *appointment (with the doctor, dentist, etc.)*
el desfile *parade*	la cita (con un amigo) *date (with a friend)*
el examen *exam*	la demostración *informative show*
	la manifestación *political demonstration/protest*

It's a Wrap

Look at your **agenda** and see what **acontecimientos** you have listed for the next two months. If you have an important event coming up that is not listed here, find it in your dictionary, then add it to your **Vocabulario personal.**

Observe the following sentences.

Hoy es jueves. Son las ocho de la mañana.
Today is Thursday. It's eight a.m.

El examen es el jueves. Es a las ocho de la mañana.
The exam is on Thursday. It's at eight a.m.

6.11 Write the equivalents.

_____	_____
The concert is on Monday.	*Today is Friday.*
_____	_____
The party's on Saturday.	*Today is Tuesday.*
_____	_____
The meeting is on Wednesday.	*The rehearsal's on Sunday.*
_____	_____
It's nine p.m.	*It's at nine a.m.*
_____	_____
It's four a.m.	*It's at four p.m.*

To Refer to Parts of the Day Without Giving a Specific Time

Compare the following sentences.

La reunión es el lunes por la mañana. *The meeting is on Monday morning.*	La reunión es el lunes a las nueve de la mañana. *The meeting is on Monday at 9 a.m.*
El partido es el sábado por la tarde. *The game is on Saturday afternoon.*	El partido es el sábado a las cuatro de la tarde. *The game is on Saturday at 4 p.m.*
La cena es el viernes por la noche. *The dinner is on Friday night.*	La cena es el viernes a las ocho de la noche. *The dinner is on Friday at 8 p.m.*

6.12　　Fill in the blanks.

When you give a specific time, you use ＿＿＿＿＿＿ **la mañana/tarde/noche,** to indicate *a.m.* or *p.m.*

Quick Tip

To give the location of an event, use *en.*

When you are referring to a period of the day without stating a time, you use ＿＿＿＿＿＿ **la mañana/tarde/noche.**

La fiesta es en la casa de Luisa.
The party is at Luisa's house.

La cena es en el restaurante Río Bravo.
The dinner is at the Rio Bravo restaurant.

El concierto es en el auditorio.
The concert is in the auditorium.

Nouns That Name Places Where Events Are Often Held

Masculino	Femenino
el cine *the movie theater*	la casa de ＿＿＿＿＿＿ *the home of ＿＿＿＿＿＿*
el teatro *the theater*	la oficina *the office*
el auditorio *the auditorium*	la escuela *the school*

Masculino	Femenino
el centro de recreo *the recreation center*	la iglesia *the church*
el estadio *the stadium*	la cafetería *the cafeteria*
el gimnasio *the gymnasium*	
el despacho *the office*	
el aula / el salón de clase *the classroom*	
el restaurante *the restaurant*	
el salón de baile *the ballroom*	

Quick Tip

If the venue of an event has an official name, give it in its original language. If it isn't a Spanish name, don't try to make it one.

6.13 Write the equivalents.

_____ *What time is it?*	_____ *It's eleven a.m.*
_____ *What time is the concert?*	_____ *It's at nine p.m.*
_____ *When is the party?*	_____ *It's on Saturday night.*
_____ *Where's the movie?*	_____ *It's at the Rialto theater.*

6.14 Practice answering the following questions in complete sentences; then listen to them on the recording, pausing it to answer them again. After you have given your answer, a speaker will give his own personal answer, which will probably not be exactly like yours. Other acceptable answers are given in the Answer Key in the Appendix.

¿Qué acontecimiento tienes para la próxima semana?

¿Qué fecha es?

¿Qué día es?

¿Es por la mañana, por la tarde o por la noche?

¿A qué hora es?

¿Dónde es?

It's a Wrap Learn the nouns that indicate events that are important to you, then add them to your **Vocabulario personal.** Practice by telling yourself aloud where, when, and at what time they will take place. Ask your Spanish-speaking friends, **¿Qué planes tienen?**

Quick Tip

The twenty-four-hour clock is commonly used in written schedules, as in television listings, museum hours, and bus, train, and airplane departures. For example:

8:00 = *a las ocho de la mañana*

20:00 = *a las ocho de la tarde*

10:30 = *a las diez y media de la mañana*

22:30 = *a las diez y media de la noche*

6.15 Write these times as you would say them in order to answer the question **¿A qué hora es la película?**

6:00 = _____

9:30 = _____

13:15 = _____

21:00 = _____

22:30 = _____

CHAPTER 7

Describing Conditions

Do I Need to Read This Chapter?

→ Do I know how to ask people how they feel, and to tell them how I feel?

→ Could I tell a doctor what my symptoms are when I'm sick?

→ Do I know the names of common ailments and serious diseases?

→ Do I know how to tell someone that he or she looks especially good?

→ Can I describe the state of my room or house?

→ Can I tell my host or cook that the food tastes good?

Is There a Friendly, Informal Way to Ask People How They Are?

When we pass people in the street or hallway, we often say "Hi, how are you?"—and only expect a "Fine, thanks, and you?" answer. It's the same in Spanish. There are two popular expressions for this purpose.

Hola, ¿qué tal?   Hola, ¿cómo está/estás?
Hi, how are you?   *Hi, how are you?*

The answer to either is:

(Muy) bien, gracias, ¿y usted/tú?
Fine, thanks, and you?

When people stop to chat, however, there are more ways to answer **¿Cómo está?**

Read the following dialogue, then follow the usual instructions.

Dialogue 12

Verónica	Rubén
Hola, amigo, ¿cómo estás? *Hello, my friend—how are you?*	Estoy muy bien, gracias. Y tú, ¿cómo estás? *I'm fine, thanks—how are you?*
Bien, pero un poquito preocupada porque mi mamá está mal. *Fine, but a little worried because my mother is doing badly.*	¿Sí? ¿Qué tiene? *Really? What's wrong with her?*
No sé qué tiene —y por eso estoy preocupada. *I don't know what's wrong with her—and that's why I'm worried.*	¿Qué síntomas tiene? *What are her symptoms?*
Tiene dolor de cabeza. No tiene energía ni apetito, y está de muy mal humor. Lo bueno es que no tiene fiebre. *She has a headache. She has no energy or appetite, and she's in a foul mood. The good thing is that she doesn't have any fever.*	Parece que está deprimida. ¿Tiene amigos aquí? *It sounds like she's depressed. Does she have any friends here?*

Verónica	Rubén
La verdad, no. En esta ciudad no tiene ningún amigo. *Actually, no. She doesn't have a single friend in this city.*	¡Con razón está mal! Exactamente como mi mamá hace unos meses. Pero ahora que tiene amigos, mi mamá está muy ocupada y contenta. *No wonder she's down—just like my mother a few months ago. But now that she has friends, my mother is busy and happy.*

The verb in **¿Cómo está?** is **estar,** and it indicates what condition someone or something is in.

Observe the following sentences.

¿Cómo estás?
How are you?

Estoy bien.
I'm fine.

¿Cómo está tu mamá?
How's your mother?

Está bien.
She's fine.

¿Cómo están ustedes?
How are you all?

Estamos bien, gracias.
We're fine, thanks.

¿Cómo están sus hijos?
How are your children?

Están bien también.
They're fine, too.

Test Yourself

7.1 Fill in the corresponding forms of **estar.**

(yo) _____

(nosotros/as) _____

(tú) _____

(Uds.) _____

(Ud.) _____

(él/ella) _____

(ellos/as) _____

Which forms have a **tilde?**

_____   _____   _____

Quick Tip

The following words that indicate condition are adverbs—they are the same for masculine, feminine, singular, and plural nouns.

bien	mal	regular / más o menos	mejor	peor
fine/OK	*not OK*	*so-so*	*better*	*worse*

7.2 To practice these forms, write the Spanish equivalents of the following.

_____ _____ _____

I'm OK.   *Are you OK?*   *We are feeling better.*

_____ _____ _____

They're worse.   *My uncle is so-so.* *The boys are in bad shape (not OK).*

7.3 Practice answering the following questions in complete sentences; then listen to them on the recording, pausing it to answer them again. After you have given your answer, a speaker will give his own personal answer, which will probably not be exactly like yours. Other acceptable answers are given in the Answer Key in the Appendix.

¿Cómo está tu mejor amigo?

¿Cómo están tus padres?

¿Cómo está tu jefe?

¿Cómo estás?

7.4 Write questions for the following answers.

Estamos bien, gracias.

Está muy mal.

Están mejor.

Estoy más o menos.

Most other words that describe a person's condition are adjectives, which do change their endings to indicate whether the noun they are describing is masculine or feminine, singular or plural.

Here are some adjectives that answer **¿Cómo está?**

Masculino y Femenino	Masculino o Femenino	
alegre *cheerful*	contento/a *happy*	cansado/a *tired*
débil *weak*	tranquilo/a *calm*	enfermo/a *sick*
fuerte *strong*	satisfecho/a *satisfied*	enojado/a *angry*
grave *in critical condition*	sano/a *in good health*	enfadado/a *angry*
	vivo/a *alive*	muerto/a *dead*
	enamorado/a *in love*	harto/a *fed up*
	listo/a *ready*	inquieto/a *anxious, nervous*
	emocionado/a *excited*	agitado/a *upset, agitated*
	intrigado/a *interested*	angustiado/a *in anguish*
	entusiasmado/a *enthusiastic*	alterado/a *upset*
	animado/a *enthusiastic, energetic*	loco/a *crazy*
	confundido/a *confused*	preocupado/a *worried*
	perdido/a *lost*	ocupado/a *busy*
		nervioso/a *nervous*

Quick Tips

estar embarazada = *to be pregnant*
tener pena = *to be embarrassed*

Quick Tip

If you want to make the adjective stronger, add *muy* or *bastante* before it.

Mi amigo está muy nervioso.
My friend is very nervous.

Estamos bastante preocupados.
We are quite worried.

If you want to make it weaker, add **un poco**.

Estoy un poco ocupada.
I'm a little busy.

It's a Wrap

Think about ten people you know and write how they are feeling, using as many of the above adjectives as you can. If you need an adjective that is not listed, look it up in your dictionary and add it to your **Vocabulario personal. ¿Cómo están estas personas?**

Describing Symptoms or Maladies in Spanish

You can use **tener** to tell what symptoms or diseases someone has. This includes certain common feelings most people experience. For example:

tener hambre *to be hungry*	tener frío *to be cold*
tener sed *to be thirsty*	tener calor *to be hot*
tener miedo *to be scared*	tener sueño *to be sleepy*

Here are some more common complaints.

tener	dolor de cabeza *a headache*	dolor de estómago *a stomachache*			
	dolor de oídos *an earache*	dolor de garganta *a sore throat*			
	dolor de muelas *a toothache*				
	un dolor en *a pain in*	el pecho, *the chest*	el cuello, *the neck*	el hombro, *the shoulder*	la pierna, etc. *the leg*

Other indications of illness.

tener	fiebre *fever*	escalofríos *chills*	dolores en todo el cuerpo *aches all over*	nauseas *nausea*
	tos *cough*	moretones *bruises*	el brazo/hombro roto *a broken arm/shoulder*	

Don't Forget

tener pena = be embarrassed
tener dolor = to have (a) pain

Quick Tip

It's not really a health complaint, but *being in a hurry* is definitely a condition and is expressed with *tener* in Spanish.

¿Tienes prisa?   Sí, tengo prisa. / No, no tengo prisa.
Are you in a hurry?   *Yes, I'm in a hurry. / No, I'm not in a hurry.*

Don't Forget

The forms of *tener:*
To refer to people who are speaking.

(yo) tengo   (nosotros) tenemos   (nosotras) tenemos

To refer to people you are speaking to.

(usted) tiene   (tú) tienes   (ustedes) tienen

To refer to people you are talking about.

(él) tiene   (ella) tiene   (ellos) tienen   (ellas) tienen

Quick Tip

The words after *tener* are nouns. To make them stronger, add *mucho/a/os/as* before them.

Tengo mucho frío.   Tiene mucha hambre.
I'm very cold.   *He's very hungry.*

Tenemos mucho miedo.   Tiene muchos dolores.
We're really scared.   *She has a lot of pains.*

Do you know anyone who is sick (or down in the dumps?) Describe his or her symptoms. **¿Cómo está? ¿Qué tiene?**

7.5 Now write questions that the following sentences answer.

Estoy bien, pero tengo hambre.

Sí, tenemos prisa.

Mi amiga está enferma.

El muchacho tiene escalofríos, pero no tiene fiebre.

No, los niños no tienen miedo.

Here are the names of some other **enfermedades**—illnesses and diseases.

Masculino	Femenino
el catarro / el resfriado *a cold*	la artritis *arthritis*
el cáncer *cancer*	la amigdalitis *tonsilitis*
el SIDA (síndrome de inmunodeficiencia adquerida) *AIDS*	la bronquitis *bronchitis*
el VIH (virus de inmunodeficiencia humana) *HIV*	la pulmonía *pneumonia*
el infarto *a heart attack*	la presión alta/baja *high/low blood pressure*

Use your dictionary to look up other diseases you want to know more about and add them to your **Vocabulario personal.** Be sure to include the **el** or **la** and put each entry in the right category.

Can I Use *estar* to Describe the Condition of Objects and Places?

Yes—it's exactly the same.

Here are some adjectives that describe common conditions.

estar	limpio *clean*	sucio *dirty*

ordenado	desordenado
neat	*messy*

arreglado	roto/descompuesto
arranged, fixed	*broken*

lleno	vacío
full	*empty*

lleno de gente	desierto
crowded	*deserted*

Here are some adjectives that describe the food—**la comida**—that has been served:

estar	caliente	frío
	piping hot	*cold*
	rico	sabroso
	delicious	*delicious, tasty*

Don't Forget

The adjectives after *estar* have endings that show whether the noun they are describing is masculine or feminine, singular or plural.

7.6 Now answer the following questions.

¿Cómo está tu casa hoy?

¿Está limpio tu coche?

¿Están sucios tus zapatos?

7.7 Complete the following.

If someone serves you delicious food, you could say:

La comida _____ .

If the food is too cold, you could say:

La comida _____ .

If you want to announce that the food is ready, you could say:

La comida _____ .

Characteristics versus Conditions

Many students of Spanish confuse **los verbos** *ser* and *estar*. The distinction is clear if you think about the *question* you are asking or answering.

¿Cómo es? asks for a description of someone or something new to you.

¿Cómo está? inquires about the health or present condition of someone or something.

Sometimes the same adjective can be used with **ser** and **estar**—but their meanings are different. Observe the following examples.

¿Cómo es? (**ser**)   ¿Cómo está? (**estar**)

ser	estar
Luisa es bonita. *Luisa is a pretty girl.*	Luisa está bonita. *Luisa looks pretty today.*
Alberto es tranquilo. *Alberto is a quiet person.*	Alberto está tranquilo. *Alberto has calmed down.*
Evita es débil. *Evita is a weakling.*	Evita está débil. *Evita is in a weak condition.*
Ramón es gordo. *Ramon is rather plump.*	Ramón está gordo. *Ramon has put on weight.*
Sarita es vieja. *Sarita is an old woman.*	Sarita está vieja. *Sarita looks old.*
Pepe es listo. *Pepe is very bright.*	Pepe está listo para el examen. *Pepe is ready for the test.*
El profesor es aburrido. *The teacher is boring.*	El profesor está aburrido. *The teacher is bored.*
Pilar es nerviosa. *Pilar is a nervous person.*	Pilar está nerviosa. *Pilar is nervous today.*
Su esposa es viva. *His wife is manipulative.*	Su esposa está viva. *His wife is alive.*
Ese hombre es malo. *That man is evil.*	Ese hombre está mal. *That man is in bad shape.*
La profesora es buena. *She's a good professor.*	La profesora está bien. *The teacher is fine.* (*isn't sick*)

Another way to look at this is to consider the following situations. If you are looking for a new job—or a new employee, friend, roommate, companion—you will ask and answer the question **¿Cómo eres?**—*What are you like?*

7.8 Then, how would you say . . . ?

I'm responsible. _____

I'm honest.   _____

After you have the job, but you can't go to work because you are sick, you might call your boss and say:

I'm sick.   _____

If your friend invites you to the movies, but you are too tired to go, you say:

I'm tired.   _____

If you go out on a date with your friend, and you get all dressed up for it, your friend (who already knows that **eres guapo/guapa**) might say:

You look handsome/beautiful. _____

Sometimes certain characteristics can cause certain conditions. Observe the following adjectives.

Characteristics (used with *ser*)	Conditions (used with *estar*)
sorprendente *surprising*	sorprendido *surprised*
emocionante *exciting*	emocionado *excited*
intrigante *intriguing*	intrigado *intrigued*
interesante *interesting*	intrigado/fascinado *interested*
impresionante *impressive*	impresionado *impressed*
fascinante *fascinating*	fascinado *fascinated*
aburrido *boring*	aburrido *bored*

7.9 Fill in the blanks with the appropriate verbs and adjectives.

Cuando la película _____ ,   las personas _____ .
When the movie   *is fascinating,*   *the people*   *are fascinated.*

El lector _____   si el libro _____ .
The reader   *is intrigued*   *if the book*   *is interesting.*

Si las noticias _____   nosotros _____ .
If the news   *is surprising,*   *we*   *are surprised.*

Los estudiantes _____   si el profesor _____ .
The students   *are bored*   *if the teacher*   *is boring.*

Are you using **ser** and **estar** without having to stop and think? Can you perform all of the activities mentioned at the beginning of this chapter? **¡Qué bueno! ¡Eso sí que es muy bueno!** Keep up the good work.

CHAPTER 8

Indicating Location

Do I Need to Read This Chapter?

→ Can I indicate where places are located on a map?

→ Am I able to indicate where the important places in my city are?

→ Do I know how to say where I am and ask others where they are?

→ Could I find something if somebody told me in Spanish where to look for it?

How to Ask Where a Place Is Located

Dialogue 13 *Una prueba de geografía.*

Maestro	Laurita
Aquí tenemos un mapa del hemisferio oeste, Laurita. ¿Estás lista para una prueba de geografía? *Here is a map of the Western Hemisphere, Laurita. Are you ready for a geography test?*	Sí, Sr. Gómez. Sé que en el hemisferio oeste están América del Norte, América del Centro y América del Sur. *Yes, Mr. Gómez. I know that the Western Hemisphere includes North America, Central America, and South America.*
La primera pregunta es: ¿Dónde está Argentina? *The first question is: Where is Argentina?*	Pues, está en el sur de América del Sur. *It's in the southern part of South America.*
¿Dónde está Canadá? *Where is Canada?*	Está en el norte de América del Norte. *It's in the northern part of North America.*
¿Qué país está en el sur de América del Norte? *What country is in the southern part of North America?*	México. México está al sur de los Estados Unidos. *It's Mexico. Mexico is south of the United States.*
Y Guatemala, ¿dónde está? *And where is Guatemala?*	Pues, está en América Central. *It's in Central America.*
¿Está Colombia en América Central? *Is Colombia in Central America?*	No. Colombia está en América del Sur. Está al sur de Panamá. *No. Colombia is in South America. It's south of Panama.*
¿Qué países están al norte de Paraguay? *What countries are to the north of Paraguay?*	Al norte de Paraguay están Bolivia y Brasil. *North of Paraguay are Bolivia and Brasil.*

Maestro	Laurita
¿Dónde está Chile? *Where is Chile?*	Chile está al oeste de Argentina y Bolivia y al sur de Perú. *Chile is to the west of Argentina and Bolivia and to the south of Peru.*
¿Qué países están en la costa del Mar Caribe? *What countries are on the coast of the Caribbean Sea?*	A ver, México, Belice, Honduras, Nicaragua, Costa Rica, Panamá, Colombia y Venezuela están en la costa del Caribe. *Let's see, Mexico, Belize, Honduras, Nicaragua, Costa Rica, Panama, Colombia, and Venezuela are on the Caribbean coast.*
¡Muy bien, Laurita! Tienes cien por ciento en la prueba de geografía. *Good, Laurita! You have 100 on the geography test.*	Gracias, Sr. Gómez. Para mí la geografía es interesante. *Thank you, Mr. Gomez. I think geography is interesting.*

8.1 Now use what you learned in the dialogue to complete the following.

Test Yourself

_____   _____
Where is Cuba?   *It's in the Caribbean.*

                                     _____
                                     It's to the south of Florida.

_____   _____
Where are Uruguay and Paraguay?   *They're in South America.*

_____   _____
Where is Nicaragua?   *It's in Central America, on the Caribbean coast.*

Don't Forget

¿De dónde eres?   Soy de _____ .
Where are you from?   *I'm from*

8.2 Practice answering the following questions in complete sentences; then listen to them on the recording, pausing it to answer them again. After you have given your answer, a speaker will give his own personal answer, which will probably not be exactly like yours. Other acceptable answers are given in the Answer Key in the Appendix.

¿De dónde eres?

¿Dónde está tu país?

¿Dónde está tu ciudad o pueblo?

¿Dónde está tu municipio?

What Are Some Other Words That Indicate Location?

From the dialogue you can see that **en** tells you exactly where a place is. You can also use the following.

está aquí *it's here*	está ahí *it's right there*	está allí *it's over there*	está cerca *it's nearby*	está lejos *it's far away*
está arriba *it's up there,* *it's upstairs*	está abajo *it's down there,* *it's downstairs*	está a la izquierda *it's to the left*	está a la derecha *it's to the right*	
está adentro *it's inside*	está afuera *it's outside*			

8.3 Now use the above expressions to complete the following.

_____   _____
I'm here.   *I'm inside.*

_____   _____
The table is right there.   *The lamp is nearby.*

_____   _____
There's a chair to the right.   *The TV is to the left.*

_____   _____
My bedroom is upstairs.   *My kitchen is downstairs.*

_____   _____
My car is outside.   *My friend's house is over there.*

Here are some nouns that name familiar places (**lugares**).

Masculino	Femenino
el banco *bank*	la calle *street*

Masculino	Femenino
el parque *park*	la biblioteca *library*
el edificio *building*	la escuela *school*
el mercado *market*	la iglesia *church*
el supermercado *supermarket*	la tienda *store*
el ayuntamiento *city hall*	la panadería *bakery*
el hotel *hotel*	la pastelería *pastry shop*
el museo *museum*	la carnicería *butcher shop*
el restaurante *restaurant*	la librería *bookstore*
el gimnasio *gym*	la ferretería *hardware store*
el hospital *hospital*	la zapatería *shoe store*
el parqueo *parking lot*	la farmacia *drugstore*
el aeropuerto *airport*	la universidad *university*
el salón de belleza *beauty salon*	la oficina de correos *post office*
el centro comercial / el mall *shopping center*	la piscina *swimming pool*
el zoológico *zoo*	la esquina *corner*
el bosque *woods*	la carretera *highway*

Masculino	Femenino
el océano *ocean*	la estación de trenes/buses/metro *train/bus/metro station*
las montañas *mountains*	la parada de autobuses *bus stop*
	la fábrica *factory*
	la playa *beach*

To tell the location of one noun in relation to another, you can use the following.

al lado de *next to*	delante de *in front of, but not facing*	detrás de *behind*	alrededor de *circling*
enfrente de *facing, across from*	debajo de *underneath*	encima de *on top of*	
sobre *on top of*	entre *between*		

8.4 Write the equivalents.

_____
The bank is across the street from the shoe store.

_____
In back of the school there's a park.

_____
There's a parking lot under the post office.

_____
There's a supermarket between the zoo and the hospital.

_____
The library is next to the bookstore.

_____
The airport is far away from the woods.

_____
The train station is close to the beach.

_____
The bakery is inside the shopping mall.

It's a Wrap

Think of your favorite areas in your own city or town, and tell where each place is located in relation to the others.

Another way to indicate where people are is to tell who they are with. Learn the following dialogue using the usual steps.

Dialogue 14   *Un muchacho perdido* 💿

Javier	Mercedes
¿Dónde está Carlitos? *Where is Carlitos?*	No sé. ¿No está con su mamá? *I don't know. Isn't he with his mother?*
No, no está con ella. *No, he's not with her.*	¿Está con su hermano? *Is he with his brother?*
No, no está con él tampoco. *No, he's not with him either.*	¿Seguro que no está contigo? *Are you sure he's not with you?*
No, claro que no está conmigo. Y tampoco está el perro. *No, of course he's not with me. And the dog isn't here either.*	Ah —ya sé dónde está. Está en el parque con su perro. *Oh—now I know where he is. He's in the park with his dog.*
Sí, tienes razón. Seguro que los dos están en el parque. *Yes, you're right. They're both at the park for sure.*	

8.5 ¿Cómo se dice. . .?
How do you say . . .?

with me   _____

with you   _____

Observe the following.

Voy contigo. *I'm going with you.*	¿Vas con él? *Are you going with him?*	Juan va con ella. *Juan is going with her.*
Vamos con usted. *We're going with you.*	Van con nosotros. *They are going with us.*	Vamos con ustedes. *We're going with you all.*
Voy con ellos. *I'm going with them.*	Ellos van conmigo. *They're going with me.*	

8.6 ¿Cómo se dice. . .?
How do you say . . .?

with him _____   with them _____

with her _____   with us _____

with you all _____

Don't Forget

You have used *dónde* with the verb *ser* for two purposes:
- to tell where someone is from: **¿de dónde es?**
- to tell the location of an event: **¿dónde es?**

To tell the location of anything else, use **estar**.

8.7 Practice answering the following questions in complete sentences; then listen to them on the recording, pausing it to answer them again. After you have given your answer, a speaker will give his own personal answer, which will probably not be exactly like yours. Other acceptable answers are given in the Answer Key in the Appendix.

¿De dónde es tu mejor amigo?

¿Dónde está él/ella?

¿Dónde estás?

¿Con quién estás?

¿Qué evento tienes para el sábado? ¿A qué hora es? ¿Dónde es?

¿Dónde está ese lugar? ¿Está cerca de tu casa?

Don't Forget

Add the names of important places in your life to your *Vocabulario personal.*

8.8 Write questions for the following answers.

No, no está conmigo.

No sé dónde están.

Es en el cine cerca de mi casa.

Está enfrente de mi casa.

Está entre Canadá y México.

Somos de Argentina.

It's a Wrap

Practice all your vocabulary words by asking and telling yourself—out loud—where different people, objects, and places are. Think of where they are in relation to other things.

◆◆◆◆◆◆◆◆◆◆◆◆◆◆◆◆◆◆◆◆◆◆◆◆◆◆◆◆◆◆◆◆◆◆◆◆

CHAPTER 9

Reporting the Weather

◆◆◆◆◆◆◆◆◆◆◆◆◆◆◆◆◆◆◆◆◆◆◆◆◆◆◆◆◆◆◆◆◆◆◆◆

Do I Need to Read This Chapter?

➡ Can I understand the weather forecast in a Spanish newspaper?

➡ Can I understand the weather forecast on a Spanish television channel?

➡ Do I know how to ask or report the current weather conditions?

➡ Do I know the names of the seasons?

➡ Can I describe the climate of my city?

Get Started

To Ask About the Weather

You can say: ¿Qué tiempo hace?   or   ¿Cómo está el tiempo hoy?
How's the weather?   *How's the weather today?*

Here are some typical answers.

Hace buen tiempo. *It's a nice day.*	Hace sol. *It's sunny.*	Hace fresco. *It's cool.*
Hace mal tiempo. *It's lousy weather.*	Hace frío. *It's cold.*	Hace viento. *It's windy.*
Hace calor. *It's hot.*	Hace 20 grados. *It's 20 degrees.*	

Some more specific answers.

Está húmedo. *It's humid.*	Está nublado. *It's cloudy.*	Está brumoso. *It's foggy.*
Está despejado. *It's clear.*	Está muy bonito. *It's beautiful.*	Está lloviendo. *It's raining.*
Está cellisqueando. *It's sleeting.*	Está granizando. *It's hailing.*	Está nevando. *It's snowing.*
Hay chubascos. *There are showers.*	Hay una tormenta. *There's a storm.*	Hay truenos. *There's thunder.*
Hay relámpagos. *There's lightning.*	Hay un tornado. *There's a tornado.*	Hay un huracán. *There's a hurricane.*
Hay un ciclón. *There's a cyclone.*	Hay un diluvio. *There's a flood.*	Hay un terremoto. *There's an earthquake.*
Hay una sequía. *There's a drought.*	Hay un maremoto. *There's a tsunami.*	

To Ask About the Temperature

Quick Tip

Temperatures are given in centigrade in Spanish-speaking countries. Rather than convert from Fahrenheit to centigrade, you may find it easier to think in terms of what is for you cold, pleasant, and hot.

¿Qué temperatura hace hoy?

0–5 grados	6–10	11–15
Hace mucho frío.	Hace frío.	Hace un poco de frío.
It's freezing.	*It's cold.*	*It's pretty cold.*

16–20	21–25	26–30
Hace fresco.	Hace buen tiempo.	Hace un poco de calor.
It's a little chilly.	*It's pleasant.*	*It's a little warm.*

31–35
Hace mucho calor.
It's really hot.

9.1 Describe the weather at the following temperatures.

◇
Test Yourself

Hace 3 grados. _____   *Hace 33 grados.* _____

Hace 23 grados. _____   *Hace 14 grados.* _____

Hace 8 grados. _____   *Hace 16 grados.* _____

Look in a Spanish-language newspaper—perhaps on the Internet—and find the weather section for today. Answer the following questions.

¿Qué temperatura hace en Santiago, Chile?
¿Qué tiempo hace?

¿Qué temperatura hace en la Ciudad de Guatemala?
¿Qué tiempo hace?

¿Qué temperatura hace en Madrid?
¿Qué tiempo hace?

¿Qué tiempo hace hoy en tu ciudad?
¿Cuál es la temperatura (más o menos) en grados centígrado?

Don't Forget

Listen to the weather report on the Spanish channel on TV. If other vocabulary is used, look it up in your dictionary and add it to your *Vocabulario personal.*

What About Seasons?

The Spanish-speaking world covers just about every possible type of climate—including temperate zones where there are four seasons, tropical regions, desert areas, mountain and other elevated areas, and coastal regions. Here are some nouns that name seasons—**las estaciones.**

Masculino	Femenino
el invierno *winter*	la primavera *spring*
el verano *summer*	la temporada lluviosa *the rainy season*
el otoño *fall*	la temporada de sequía *the dry season*

Read, listen to, and learn the following dialogue using the usual steps.

Dialogue 15 🔊

Maria	El tío de Maria
Hola, tío Pedro. *Hello, Uncle Pedro.*	Hola, Maria. Bienvenida a Argentina y a nuestra casa. *Hello, Maria. Welcome to Argentina and to our house.*

Maria	El tío de Maria
Hace mucho frío ¡y estamos en pleno junio! *It's so cold—and it's the middle of June!*	Sí, Maria, pero no estamos en Nueva York, sino en Buenos Aires. *Yes, Maria, but we're not in New York; we're in Buenos Aires.*
Y eso—¿qué? *So what?*	Bueno, estamos en el hemisferio del sur. En Argentina hace frío en junio, julio y agosto, porque es el invierno. *Well, we're in the Southern Hemisphere. In Argentina it's cold in June, July, and August because it's winter.*
Entonces, el verano es en... *Then summer is in ...*	Sí, diciembre, enero y febrero. *Yes—December, January, and February.*
Pero, ¡qué raro! La Navidad y el Año Nuevo son en el verano. *That's really weird! Christmas and New Year's are in the summer.*	Exacto —y tenemos las flores de primavera en septiembre, octubre y noviembre. *Exactly—and we have spring flowers in September, October, and November.*
Y las hojas pintadas del otoño en marzo, abril y mayo. *And autumn leaves in March, April, and May.*	Así es. Pero fíjate que hay otros climas. Por ejemplo, en Guatemala, siempre es primavera. Hace buen tiempo durante todo el año. *That's right. But remember that there are other climates, too. For example, in Guatemala it's always spring. It's nice all year.*
Qué interesante. ¿Qué otros climas hay? *That's interesting. What other climates are there?*	Bueno, en la selva llueve mucho. En el desierto no llueve casi nunca. En las montañas hace calor durante el día y hace frío por la noche. *Well, in the jungle it rains a lot. In the desert it hardly ever rains. In the mountains it's hot during the day and cold at night.*

Quick Tips

Llueve mucho. = *It rains a lot.* Está lloviendo. = *It's raining.* No nieva nunca. = *It never snows.* Está nevando. = *It's snowing.*

9.2 Write the equivalents.

_____   _____

It's pleasant in the spring and fall.   *It's hot in the summer.*

_____   _____

It's cold in the winter.   *It rains a lot.*

_____   _____

It never snows.   *It's nice all year.*

Practice answering the following questions in complete sentences; then listen to them on the recording, pausing it to answer them again. After you have given your answer, a speaker will give his own personal answer, which will probably not be exactly like yours. Other acceptable answers are given in the Answer Key in the Appendix.

 ¿Cómo es el clima de tu país?

¿Hay estaciones?

¿Llueve mucho? ¿Cuándo?

¿En qué estación es tu cumpleaños?

¿Qué tiempo hace el día de tu cumpleaños (generalmente)?

It's a Wrap

Think about your favorite events throughout the year. Talk to yourself about them out loud. What seasons are they in? What's the weather like then? Do you have parties? When? Where? You may want to review Chapter 6 at this point. Then ask your Spanish-speaking friends about the climate in the countries they or their families are from, and about the events they celebrate at different seasons. If you can do this, you've made a lot of progress. **¡Muy bien!**

CHAPTER 10

Giving Facts and Describing Usual Activities

Do I Need to Read This Chapter?

➡ Can I ask people where they live or work, and tell the same about myself?

➡ Can I describe what I do at work, what I do for fun, what I read, eat, wear, how many hours I sleep—in short, describe my day-to-day activities?

➡ Can I write a paragraph telling how my life differs from that of my friends?

➡ Do I know how to look up an action word in the dictionary—and then use it correctly?

So far we have been concentrating on nouns and adjectives. While learning them, you have been using four verbs.

ser   for identifying, telling origin, describing, telling time, and giving the time, place, and location of events

estar   for telling present conditions and for giving the location of people, places, and things

tener   for giving certain descriptions, telling age, telling certain present conditions, and for telling what things people have in their possession

querer for telling what people want

Test Yourself

10.1 See if you can write the conjugations of these verbs. If necessary, go back and review the previous chapters.

	ser	estar	tener	querer
(yo)	_____	_____	_____	_____
(tú)	_____	_____	_____	_____
(Ud./él/ella)	_____	_____	_____	_____
(nosotros/as)	_____	_____	_____	_____
(Uds./ellos/as)	_____	_____	_____	_____

I've Heard That There Are So Many Irregular Verbs in Spanish That It's Not Possible to Learn Them All

It's true that nothing could be more boring—or counterproductive—than memorizing long lists of verbs and their spelling changes. We will approach these important words differently—introducing them according to how they are used and then practicing them in context. Follow the steps in this chapter very carefully, keep practicing, and you will develop a good understanding of how verbs work in Spanish.

To Find Spanish Verbs in the Dictionary

Verbs are listed in the dictionary according to their infinitive forms. Observe the following infinitive forms.

trabajar	comer	vivir
work	*eat*	*live*

hablar	aprender	escribir
talk	*learn*	*write*

escuchar	leer	salir
listen	*read*	*go out*

10.2 Fill in the blanks.

The final letters of the infinitive form of a verb are either _____ ,

_____ , or _____ .

Removing those last two letters and adding others is the way Spanish indicates *who* is doing the action and *when* it takes place. In this chapter we will explore the ways to describe activity that takes place at the present time, on a regular basis. For this purpose, Spanish uses **el tiempo presente.**

Get Started

Read, listen to, and learn the following dialogue using the usual steps.

Dialogue 16   *La vida de una estudiante.*

Diego	Cristina
Díme, Cristina—ahora que eres estudiante de la universidad, ¿cómo es tu vida? *Tell me, Cristina—now that you're a college student, what's your life like?*	Ay, Diego, es muy interesante. Tengo un horario lleno de actividades. *Well, Diego, it's really interesting. I have a busy schedule.*
¿Qué haces todos los días? *What do you do every day?*	La verdad, cada día es distinto. *Actually, every day is different.*
Es muy diferente de la escuela secundaria, ¿verdad? *It's really different from high school, right?*	Sí. Por ejemplo, tengo algunas clases los lunes y miércoles, otras los martes y jueves —y la clase de español los martes, jueves y viernes. *Yes. For example, I have some classes on Mondays and Wednesdays, others on Tuesdays and Thursdays, and Spanish class on Tuesdays, Thursdays, and Fridays.*

Diego	Cristina
¿Qué hacen ustedes en la clase de español? *What do you all do in Spanish class?*	Bueno, por supuesto, hablamos español. Escuchamos a la profesora y luego practicamos las formas nuevas. *Well, of course, we speak Spanish. We listen to the teacher and then we practice the new forms.*
¿Hay mucha tarea? *Is there a lot of homework?*	Claro. Memorizamos el vocabulario nuevo y luego contestamos muchas preguntas. *Naturally. We memorize new vocabulary and then answer a lot of questions.*
¿Cuándo la haces? *When do you do it?*	Hago la tarea en la tarde. Paso por lo menos tres horas cada día en la biblioteca. *I do my homework in the afternoon. I spend at least three hours in the library every day.*
Entonces, ¡trabajas todo el tiempo! *So you work all the time!*	Estudio mucho, sí, pero también paso tiempo con mis amigos. Hablamos de todo, escuchamos música, bailamos . . . En fin, la pasamos muy bien. *I study a lot, yes. But I also spend time with my friends. We talk about everything, listen to music, dance . . . Really, we have a good time.*
Pero no descansas nunca. *But you never rest.*	Eso sí es la verdad. No descanso nunca. *That's the truth. I never rest.*

Here are three verbs whose infinitives end in **-ar**.

trabajar	hablar	escuchar
work	*speak/talk*	*listen*

Observe the following sentences.

Trabajo mucho.	Trabajamos mucho.
I work a lot.	*We work a lot.*

Hablo español.	Hablamos español.
I speak Spanish.	*We speak Spanish.*

Escucho la radio.   Escuchamos la radio.
I listen to the radio.   *We listen to the radio.*

10.3 Now describe the pattern.

Find the stem of the verb by removing the **-ar** ending from the infinitive.

If the person who performs the action is the speaker him- or herself (**yo**), add _____ .

If the performer is the speaker plus one or more others (**nosotros/nosotras**), add _____ .

Observe these sentences.

Juan trabaja mucho.   Juan y Paco trabajan mucho.
Juan works a lot.   *Juan and Paco work a lot.*

Juanita habla español.   Juanita y Elena hablan español.
Juanita speaks Spanish.   *Juanita and Elena speak Spanish.*

Juan escucha la radio.   Juan y Juanita escuchan la radio.
Juan listens to the radio.   *Juan and Juanita listen to the radio.*

10.4 Now describe the pattern.

To indicate that another person performs the activity:

If it is one other person (**él/ella**), add _____ to the stem.

If it is more than one other person (**ellos/ellas**), add _____ .

Observe these sentences.

Trabaja mucho.   Trabajan mucho.
*You (**usted**) work a lot.*   *You all work a lot.*

Trabajas mucho.
*You (**tú**) work a lot.*

10.5 Now describe the pattern.

To remark to another person or people that they perform an activity.

If it is one person, whom you would call **usted,** add _____ to the stem.

If it is a person you would call **tú,** add _____ .

If it is more than one person (**ustedes**), add _____ .

Don't Forget

Only use the subject pronouns—*yo, nosotros, tú, usted, ustedes, él, ella, ellos, ellas*—if they are absolutely necessary for clarification or if you want to emphasize them. A conjugated verb can be a complete sentence:

Here is a list of infinitives of **-ar** verbs that describe popular activities.

bailar *dance*	contestar *answer*	lavar *wash*	practicar *practice*
cantar *sing*	escuchar *listen*	limpiar *clean*	preguntar *ask questions*
cocinar *cook*	estudiar *study*	manejar *drive*	trabajar *work*
comprar *shop/buy*	hablar *speak/talk*	pasar tiempo *spend time*	usar *use*

10.6 Now complete the following.

I dance	*we sing*	*you cook*	*they buy*
she answers	*he listens*	*we clean*	*I ask*
you use	*I work*	*he washes*	*she talks*
they drive	*we spend time*	*you study*	*I practice*

To Ask Questions About People's Activities

To make a yes-or-no question, simply put question marks around the statement.

Estudias mucho.   ¿Estudias mucho?
You study a lot.   *Do you study a lot?*

Pepe habla inglés.   ¿Pepe habla inglés? / ¿Habla Pepe inglés?
Pepe speaks English.   *Does Pepe speak English?*

10.7 Complete the following.

_____	_____	_____
Do you speak Spanish?	*Does María work?*	*Do Ana and her sister drive?*

_____	_____	_____
Do you all cook?	*Do we talk a lot?*	*Does Enrique dance?*

10.8 Practice answering the following questions in complete sentences; then listen to them on the recording, pausing it to answer them again. After you have given your answer, a speaker will give his own personal answer, which will probably not be exactly like yours. Other acceptable answers are given in the Answer Key in the Appendix.

¿Estudias español?

¿Hablan tú y tu mejor amigo mucho por teléfono?

¿Trabaja tu mejor amigo?

¿Cantan tus amigos?

10.9 Write questions for the following answers.

Sí, lavamos los coches.

Sí, escucha la música *rock*.

No, no uso la computadora en casa.

No, no contesta.

To Ask for Details About People's Activities

Use the question words you have already learned with the appropriate conjugated verbs.

Consider the following question-answer exchanges.

Questions Directed to One Person	Answer in the *yo* Form
¿Qué hace usted / haces todos los días? *What do you do every day?*	Trabajo. *I work.*
¿Dónde trabaja/trabajas? *Where do you work?*	Trabajo en el centro. *I work downtown.*

Questions Directed to One Person	Answer in the *yo* Form
	Trabajo para la Compañía XYZ. *I work for the XYZ Company.*
¿Con quién trabaja/trabajas? *Who do you work with?*	Trabajo con mi hermano. *I work with my brother.*

Questions Directed to Two or More People	Answer in the *nosotros* Form
¿Cuándo trabajan ustedes? *When do you all work?*	Trabajamos los días de la semana, de lunes a viernes. *We work on weekdays from Monday to Friday.*
¿A qué hora trabajan? *What time do you work?*	Trabajamos de las ocho hasta las cinco. *We work from eight until five.*

Questions About One Other Person	Answer in the *él/ella* Form
¿Trabaja José con ustedes? *Does Jose work with you all?*	Sí, trabaja con nosotros. *Yes, he works with us.*
¿Con qué frecuencia trabaja? *How often does he work?*	Trabaja tres días a la semana. *He works three days a week.*
¿Cómo trabaja José? *How does Jose work?*	José trabaja muy bien. *Jose works very well.*

Questions About Two or More People	Answer in the *ellos/ellas* Form
¿Trabajan Ernesto y Magaly con ustedes? *Do Ernesto and Magaly work with you all?*	No, ya no trabajan aquí. *No, they don't work here anymore.*
¿Dónde trabajan? *Where do they work?*	Trabajan en otro lugar. *They work at another place.*
¿Cómo trabajan? *How do they work?*	Trabajan muy mal. *They work very badly.*

Practice the same question-answer sequences, using **estudiar** and **cocinar**. Here are some alternative answers to use with information questions.

¿Dónde? *Where?*	en la ciudad, en la casa, *in the city at home* en un restaurante, en el mercado, *at a restaurant at the market* afuera, no [*verb*] en ningún lugar *outside nowhere/not anywhere*
¿Cuándo? *When?*	todos los días, los jueves, siempre, *every day on Thursdays always* los fines de semana, no [*verb*] nunca *on weekends never*
¿A qué hora? *What time?*	a la una, a las dos y media de la tarde *at one o'clock at two-thirty p.m.*
¿Con qué frecuencia? *How often?*	dos veces al día, cuatro veces al mes, *twice a day four times a month* una vez a la semana, mucho, poco *once a week a lot very little* a veces, todos los días *sometimes every day* a menudo, todo el tiempo *often all the time*
¿Para quién? *Who for?*	para el Sr. Martínez / la Compañía XZ *for [name of a person or organization]* no [*verb*] para nadie *not for anybody*
¿Con quién(es)? *Who with?*	con Miguel / Joaquín y Sara *with [name of a person or people]* no [*verb*] con nadie, solo/a *with nobody alone*
¿Cómo? *How?*	bien, mal, rápido, lento, con cuidado, *well badly fast slowly carefully* duro, con orgullo, con entusiasmo, *hard proudly enthusiastically* sin esmero, sin entusiasmo *carelessly without enthusiasm*

Are There Other Ways to Say How Something Is Done?

Observe the following sentences.

Soy orgulloso.	Trabajo orgullosamente.
I am proud.	*I work proudly.*
Jaime está contento.	Jaime escucha la radio contentamente.
Jaime is content.	*Jaime listens contentedly to the radio.*
Marta es paciente.	Marta espera pacientemente.
Marta is patient.	*Marta waits patiently.*
Somos muy rápidos.	Cocinamos rápidamente.
We are fast.	*We cook fast.*
Los niños están alegres.	Los niños cantan alegremente.
The children are happy.	*The children sing happily.*

10.10 Describe the pattern.

To form an *adverb*—to describe how an action is performed—start with the
_____ form of an adjective and add _____ .

10.11 Now write the equivalents.

_____   _____

Ana Maria waits nervously.   *Horacio speaks in a vulgar manner.*

_____   _____

They drive slowly.   *She works independently.*

_____   _____

Carlos answers kindly.   *I work happily.*

Quick Tip

Some adverbs can alternatively be stated in the masculine singular form of an adjective. The most common of these are:

rápido	lento	despacio	duro
fast	*slow*	*slow*	*hard*

Don't Forget

Add to your *Vocabulario personal* any adverbs you need that describe the way something is done.

Quick Tip

If you don't know the answer to a question, just say *No sé* and repeat the question. For example:

¿Dónde estudia tu amigo?	No sé dónde estudia.
Where does your friend study?	*I don't know where he studies.*
¿Cuándo almuerzan ellos?	No sé cuándo almuerzan.
When do they eat lunch?	*I don't know when they eat lunch.*

If it's a yes-or-no question, say **No sé si** and repeat the question.

For example:

¿Estudia química Juan?	No sé si estudia química.
Does Juan study chemistry?	*I don't know if he studies chemistry.*

Quick Tip

Omit the *el* or *la* after *estudiar*. *Estudio música.*

Here is a list of subjects you might want to use with **estudiar**. Look up any others you need and add them to your **Vocabulario personal.**

Masculino	Femenino
los idiomas *languages*	la medicina *medicine*
el periodismo *journalism*	la pintura *painting*
el baile *dance*	la política *politics*
	las artes liberales *liberal arts*
	la historia *history*

Masculino	Femenino
	la economía *economics*
	la geografía *geography*
	la lingüística *linguistics*
	la informática *computer science*
	la ingeniería *engineering*
	la música *music*
	la ciencia *science*
	las matemáticas *math*
	las leyes *law*

This is a lot to learn. Review it several times, and practice the questions and answers by talking to yourself aloud. Talk about yourself, your friends, your family, the people you work with—you can never practice too much!

Am I Ready to Use All *-ar* Verbs Now?

First look at another regular pattern that many verbs follow. Observe the following.

empezar (ie) *start, begin*	pensar (ie) *think*	jugar (ue) *play*	almorzar (ue) *eat lunch*
empiezo *I start*	pienso *I think*	juego *I play*	almuerzo *I eat lunch*
empiezas *you start*	piensas *you think*	juegas *you play*	almuerzas *you eat lunch*
empieza *you start* *he starts* *she starts*	piensa *you think* *he thinks* *she thinks*	juega *you play* *he plays* *she plays*	almuerza *you eat lunch* *he eats lunch* *she eats lunch*

empezar (ie)	pensar (ie)	jugar (ue)	almorzar (ue)
start, begin	*think*	*play*	*eat lunch*
empiezan	piensan	juegan	almuerzan
you all start	*you all think*	*you all play*	*you all eat lunch*
they start	*they think*	*they play*	*they eat lunch*
empezamos	pensamos	jugamos	almorzamos
we start	*we think*	*we play*	*we eat lunch*

10.12 Now describe the pattern.

When the dictionary indicates (_____) or (_____) after an infinitive, that combination replaces the vowel closest to the end of the stem in all conjugated forms except _____ .

10.13 Fill in the forms.

comenzar (ie)	recordar (ue)
start, begin	*remember*

_____	_____
I begin	*I remember*
_____	_____
you begin	*you remember*
_____	_____
you begin / he / she begins	*you remember / he / she remembers*
_____	_____
you all / they begin	*you all / they remember*
_____	_____
we begin	*we remember*

Quick Tips

recordar = *remember*   grabar = *record* (*make a tape*)

10.14 Answer these questions in complete sentences.

     ¿A qué hora empiezan tus clases?

     ¿Qué juegan tú y tus amigos?

     ¿Con quién almuerza tu mejor amigo?

     ¿Recuerdas el nombre de tu primera maestra en la escuela?

10.15 Write questions for the following answers.

     Juega tenis. / Juega al tenis.

     Almorzamos a las dos.

     Comienza a las siete y media.

     No, no recuerdo.

Here is a list of verbs that you can use to describe what you or other people do on a regular basis.

arreglar cosas *fix things*	ganar premios *win prizes*	navegar en el Internet *surf the Internet*
buscar cosas *look for things*	ganar dinero *earn money*	olvidar *forget*
caminar en el parque *walk in the park*	gastar dinero *spend money*	opinar *give your opinion*
cenar *eat dinner*	hablar por teléfono *talk on the telephone*	participar en un grupo *participate in a group*
conversar *chat*	jugar (ue) fútbol *play soccer*	practicar un deporte *participate in a sport*
desayunar *eat breakfast*	jugar (ue) cartas *play cards*	protestar en la calle *protest in the street*
dibujar *draw pictures*	llegar tarde *arrive late*	soñar (ue) durante el día *dream during the day*
encontrar (ue) cosas *find things*	llegar temprano *arrive early*	tocar un instrumento *play an instrument*
fabricar cosas *make things*	llevar ropa llamativa *wear flashy clothes*	trabajar afuera *work outside*
	llevar ropa conservadora *wear conservative clothes*	votar en las elecciones *vote*

Practice the verbs by asking and answering these questions.

¿_____ ?　　　　¿Cuándo (<u>verb</u>)?　　　　¿A qué hora (<u>verb</u>)?
Do you (<u>verb</u>)?　　　　*When do you _____ ?*　　*What time do you _____ ?*

¿Con qué frecuencia (<u>verb</u>)?　¿Con quién (<u>verb</u>)?　　¿Dónde (<u>verb</u>)?
How often do you _____ ?　　*Who do you _____*　　*Where do you _____ ?*
　　　　　　　　　　　　　　　with?

¿Cómo?
How (well) do you (<u>verb</u>)?

Ask your Spanish-speaking friends about their regular activities and tell them about yours. And take a minute to pat yourself on the back. You are speaking quite a bit of Spanish. **Ya hablas bastante español. ¡Estupendo!**

Using Verbs Whose Infinitives End in -er

Read, listen to, and memorize the following dialogue.

Dialogue 17   Estar en forma 💿

Oye, amigo, veo que estás en forma. ¿Cómo lo haces? *Hey, pal, I see you're in good shape. How do you do it?*	Bueno, como bien, eso es, muchas frutas y verduras, y muy poca grasa. Y bebo ocho vasos de agua cada día. *Well, I eat well—lots of fruits and vegetables and very little fat. And I drink eight glasses of water every day.*
¿Haces ejercicio? *Do you exercise?*	Claro. Corro cinco kilómetros en la mañana antes de ir al trabajo, y por la tarde voy al gimnasio. *Yes indeed. I run five Ks in the morning before I go to work, and I go to the gym in the evening.*
¡Con razón estás en forma! Ahora comprendo la importancia de comer bien y hacer ejercicio. *No wonder you're in such good shape! Now I see the importance of eating well and doing exercise.*	¡Tú no haces nada! Creo que necesitas hacer un programa. ¿Por qué no me acompañas al gimnasio esta tarde? *You don't do anything! I think you need a program. Why don't you come to the gym with me this evening?*
Gracias, amigo. Tienes razón. *Thanks, pal. You're right.*	Entonces, ¿nos vemos aquí a las cinco? *Then shall we meet here at five o'clock?*

Observe the following.

aprender *learn*	leer *read*	comer *eat*
aprendo *I learn*	leo *I read*	como *I eat*
aprendes *you learn*	lees *you read*	comes *you eat*
aprende *you learn* *he/she learns*	lee *you read* *he/she reads*	come *you eat* *he/she eats*
aprendemos *we learn*	leemos *we read*	comemos *we eat*
aprenden *you all learn* *they learn*	leen *you all read* *they read*	comen *you all eat* *they eat*

10.16 Now write the pattern.

To conjugate the verbs whose infinitives end in **-er,** first take off _____ , then add to the stem the following endings:

(yo) _____   (nosotros/as) _____

(tú) _____   (Uds.) _____

(Ud./él/ella) _____   (ellos/as) _____

Here are a few more common verbs that follow this pattern.

beber	comprender	recoger
drink	*understand*	*pick up*
creer	escoger	responder
believe	*choose*	*answer*
correr	esconder	vender
run	*hide*	*sell*

10.17 Write the following forms.

_____   _____   _____
we answer   *she doesn't understand*   *they sell*

_____   _____   _____
I believe   *Do you run?*   *he drinks*

Quick Tip

Four ways to express your opinion:

Creo que sí.   Creo que no.   Lo creo.   No lo creo.
I think so.   *I don't think so.*   *I believe it.*   *I don't believe it.*

Here are some nouns you might find useful for answering the following questions.

¿Qué lee?*
What do you read?

Masculino	Femenino
el libro *book*	la literatura *literature*
el informe *report*	la novela *novel*
el reportaje *newspaper report*	la poesía *poetry*
el artículo *article*	la revista *magazine*
el cuento *short story*	la tesis *thesis*
el poema *poem*	la carta *letter*
el comentario *commentary*	

¿Qué bebe?*
What do you drink?

Masculino	Femenino
el agua *water*	la leche *milk*
el jugo *juice*	la cerveza *beer*
el vino *wine*	la limonada *lemonade*
los refrescos *soft drinks*	la soda *soda*
el café *coffee*	
el té *tea*	

¿Qué come?*
What do you eat?

Masculino		Femenino	
el queso *cheese*	el pan *bread*	la carne *meat*	las tortillas *pancakes, omelettes*
el yogur *yogurt*	el cereal *cereal*	la carne de res *beef*	las papayas *papayas*
el helado *ice cream*	el arroz *rice*	las verduras *vegetables*	
el pescado *fish*	el pollo *chicken*	las papas *potatoes*	
los mariscos *shellfish*	el pavo *turkey*	la ensalada *salad*	
los huevos *eggs*	los mangos *mangoes*	las frutas *fruits*	

¿Qué come?*
What do you eat?

Masculino		Femenino
el puerco *pork*	los tomates *tomatoes*	las naranjas *oranges*
los frijoles *beans*	el postre *dessert*	las manzanas *apples*
el plátano *banana*	los dulces *candy*	la piña *pineapple*
el aguacate *avocado*		las uvas *grapes*

* Use the article (**el, la, los, las**) after **leer**; leave it out after **beber** and **comer.**

10.18 Answer the following questions in complete sentences.

¿Cuándo lees el periódico?

¿Corre tu mejor amigo?

¿Qué comen tú y tus amigos en un restaurante?

¿Dónde venden pescado fresco en tu ciudad?

10.19 Write a question for each of the following answers.

No sé a qué hora comen.

Sí, comprendo.

Corro por la mañana.

Venden el periódico en la calle.

If your favorite food or beverage isn't on this list, look it up in a dictionary and add it to your **Vocabulario personal.** Practice the names of different types of food by asking yourself what you eat at different times of the day, where you eat certain things, and who you eat with. Now observe the following verbs.

entender (ie) *understand*	perder (ie) *lose*	volver (ue) *return, go (come) back*	resolver (ue) *solve*
entiendo *I understand*	pierdo *I lose*	vuelvo *I return*	resuelvo *I solve*
entiendes *you understand*	pierdes *you lose*	vuelves *you return*	resuelves *you solve*
entiende *you understand* *he/she understands*	pierde *you lose* *he/she loses*	vuelve *you return* *he/she returns*	resuelve *you solve* *he/she solves*
entienden *you all understand* *they understand*	pierden *you all lose* *they lose*	vuelven *you all return* *they return*	resuelven *you all solve* *they solve*
entendemos *we understand*	perdemos *we lose*	volvemos *we return*	resolvemos *we solve*

10.20 Write the pattern.

When the dictionary indicates (_____) or (_____) after an infinitive, those letters replace the _____ vowel of the stem in all conjugated forms except _____ .

Do you remember the verb **querer**? Does it follow this pattern? _____ What letters would you find in parentheses after it in a dictionary? _____

10.21 Write the equivalents.

_____ *I understand*	_____ *she comes back*	_____ *they want*
_____ *we lose*	_____ *he solves*	_____ *I read*
_____ *he sells*	_____ *we want*	_____ *Do you understand?*
_____ *they believe*	_____ *she answers*	_____ *I go back*

Quick Tip

perder has two meanings: (1) lose something and (2) miss an event, a bus, or a train.

Pedro siempre pierde sus anteojos.
Pedro always loses his glasses.

Pedro nunca pierde una fiesta.
Pedro never misses a party.

Observe the following.

	ver *see*	saber *know (information)*	hacer *do*	poner *put*	traer *bring*	conocer *know (people)*
(yo)	veo	sé	hago	pongo	traigo	conozco
(tú)	ves	sabes	haces	pones	traes	conoces
(Ud./él/ella)	ve	sabe	hace	pone	trae	conoce
(Uds./ellos/as)	ven	saben	hacen	ponen	traen	conocen
(nosotros/as)	vemos	sabemos	hacemos	ponemos	traemos	conocemos

10.22 Complete the following.

These verbs follow the usual patterns except in the _____ form.

10.23 Write the equivalents.

_____	_____	_____
we bring	*they know (something)*	*I do*
_____	_____	_____
she sees	*I put*	*he knows (somebody)*
_____	_____	_____
I don't know (information)	*we see*	*Do you know? (information)*
_____	_____	_____
I know (people)	*Do you bring . . . ?*	*I see*

Quick Tip

In English, we use the verb *know* for both information and people. Spanish uses two different words:

saber for information: Sé su número de teléfono.
I know her telephone number.

No sé dónde está.
I don't know where she is.

conocer for acquaintance of people or places; if it is a person or people, always add **a**:

Conozco a Juan.
I know Juan.

Conozco Nueva York.
I've been in New York.

Observe these verbs.

	parecer *seem*	merecer *deserve*	obedecer *obey*
(yo)	parezco	merezco	obedezco

10.24 You can guess that these work just like **conocer**. Write the equivalents.

_____   _____   _____
She seems nice.   *We deserve money.*   *I don't know Monica.*

_____   _____   _____
They obey.   *I don't obey.*   *He seems bored.*

10.25 Answer the following.

¿Qué pierdes a veces?

¿A cuántas personas que hablan español conoces?

¿Qué leen tú y tus amigos?

¿Qué comen las personas en un restaurante mexicano?

¿Sabe tu mejor amigo dónde estás?

10.26 Write questions for the following answers.

Sí, ella sabe la fecha de mi cumpleaños.

No conozco a nadie.

Volvemos a la oficina a las dos.

Siempre come en casa con su familia.

No, no conozco Bolivia.

Now you have seen and practiced the **-er** verbs. Review this section when you need to and keep asking questions like **¿Qué hace? ¿Dónde come? ¿Cuándo vuelve? ¿A quién conoce? ¿Qué sabe de . . . ?**

Using Verbs Whose Infinitives End in *-ir*

Read, listen to, and learn the following dialogue using the usual steps.

Dialogue 18   Un consejo.

Hermano, tengo un gran problema. Le escribo muchos emails a mi novia, pero ella nunca me contesta. *Brother, I've got a big problem. I write a lot of emails to my girlfriend, but she never answers.*	¿Estás seguro que ella recibe tus mensajes? *Are you sure she's receiving your messages?*
Pues, creo que sí. Creo que tengo la dirección correcta. *I guess so. I think I have the right address.*	¿Sabes si ella abre su correo? *Do you know if she opens her email?*
No, no lo sé. *No, I really don't know.*	¿Sabes dónde vive? *Do you know where she lives?*
Sí, vive en la Calle Mercedes, 4B. *Yes, she lives at 4B Mercedes Street.*	Entonces, tengo una idea. ¿Por qué no le escribes una carta tradicional? Es mucho más romántico. *Then I have an idea. Why don't you send her an old-fashioned letter? It's much more romantic.*
Sí, es una buena idea. Las chicas prefieren las cartas verdaderas. Eres un genio. *Yes, that's a good idea. Girls prefer real letters. You're a genius.*	Un genio, no. Pero conozco bien a las chicas. *No, not a genius. But I do understand girls.*

10.27   Observe the forms of the first verb, then complete the chart.

	escribir *write*	recibir *receive*	abrir *open*	vivir *live*	preferir (ie) *prefer*
(yo)	escribo	_____	_____	_____	_____
(tú)	escribes	_____	_____	_____	_____

	escribir *write*	recibir *receive*	abrir *open*	vivir *live*	preferir (ie) *prefer*
(Ud./él/ella) escribe	_____	_____	_____	_____	
(Uds./ellos/as) escriben	_____	_____	_____	_____	
(nosotros/as) escribimos	_____	_____	_____	_____	

10.28 Now write the pattern.

To conjugate a verb whose infinitive ends in **-ir,** first take off the _____ , then

add _____ to speak about oneself (**yo**)

_____ to speak about oneself and other people together (**nosotros/as**)

_____ to speak to one good friend (**tú**)

_____ to speak to someone of a different social group (**usted**)

_____ to speak to more than one person (**ustedes**)

_____ to speak about one other person (**él/ella**)

_____ to speak about more than one other person (**ellos/as**)

If letters appear in parentheses after the infinitive, those letters replace the _____ vowel in the stem in all forms except _____ .

Here are some more **-ir** verbs. Notice that stem-changing indications for these can be (**ue**), (**ie**), or (**i**).

| asistir a *attend* | servir (i) *serve* | mentir (ie) *lie (deceive)* | dormir (ue) *sleep* | morir (ue) *die* |

10.29 Write the equivalents.

_____	_____	_____
she sleeps	*we attend*	*he serves*
_____	_____	_____
I don't lie	*they don't die*	*we sleep*
_____	_____	_____
Do you serve?	*she attends*	*we serve*

10.30 Practice answering the following questions in complete sentences; then listen to them on the recording, pausing it to answer them again. After you have given your answer, a speaker will give his own personal answer, which will probably not be exactly like yours. Other acceptable answers are given in the Answer Key in the Appendix.

¿Recibes muchas cartas?

¿Cuando escriben email tus amigos?

¿Dónde vives?

¿Cuántas horas duermes por la noche?

¿Quién sirve la comida en tu casa?

¿Con quién vive tu mejor amigo?

¿Asistes a una clase de español?

¿Abres todo el email que recibes?

¿Es verdad que las chicas prefieren las cartas verdaderas?

Y tú, ¿prefieres el email o las cartas verdaderas?

10.31 Write questions for the following answers.

El niño no duerme bien.

Preferimos helado de chocolate.

El abuelo muere al final de la película.

Sí, creo que el novio miente.

Sirven la cena a las ocho de la noche.

No sé a qué colegio asiste ella.

Mi hermana vive en Chicago con su esposo y sus hijos.

Observe the following verb.

salir ***go out***	
Salgo con mis amigos. *I go out with my friends.*	Salimos a las ocho. *We go out at eight.*
Sales mucho. *You go out a lot.*	Salen poco. *You all go out very little.*
Sale con María. *He goes out with Maria.*	Salen con nosotras. *They go out with us.*

10.32 Complete the following.

salir is conjugated just like other **-ir** verbs except in the _____ form.

Here are some other uses of **salir**.

Salgo de la oficina a las seis.
I leave the office at six.

¿A qué hora sales para la ciudad?
What time do you leave for the city?

10.33 Answer the following questions.

¿Con quién sales a veces?

¿A qué hora sales de tu casa por la mañana?

¿Para dónde sales en la tarde?

Observe these two verbs.

	decir (i) ***say***	venir (ie) ***come***
(yo)	digo	vengo
(tú)	dices	vienes
(Ud./él/ella)	dice	viene
(Uds./ellos/as)	dicen	vienen
(nosotros/as)	decimos	venimos

10.34 Complete the following.

The verbs **decir** and **venir** follow the usual patterns except in the _____ form.

Observe the following sentences.

Digo: Es una buena idea.
I say, "It's a good idea."

Digo que es una buena idea.
I say (that) it's a good idea.

Juan dice: No está bien.
Juan says, "It's not OK."

Juan dice que no está bien.
Juan says (that) it's not OK.

Verónica dice: Sí.
Veronica says, "Yes."

Verónica dice que sí.
Veronica says yes.

Sus padres dicen: No.
Her parents say, "No."

Sus padres dicen que no.
Her parents say no.

10.35 Complete the following.

To indicate the meaning *say,* unless it's a direct quote, use _____ after **decir**.

10.36 Answer the following questions.

¿Qué dices de tu clase?

¿Qué dice tu profesor de tu español?

A few verbs end in **-uir** and have a change in spelling. Observe these two.

contribuir	distribuir
Contribuyo algo. *I contribute something.*	Distribuyo los documentos. *I distribute the documents.*
¿Qué contribuyes? *What do you contribute?*	¿Cúando los distribuyes? *When do you distribute them?*
Él no contribuye nada. *He doesn't contribute anything.*	Ella distribuye los documentos. *She distributes the documents.*
Contribuyen mucho. *They contribute a lot.*	No distribuyen nada. *They don't distribute anything.*
Contribuimos dinero. *We contribute money.*	Distribuimos los documentos. *We distribute the documents.*

10.37 Write the pattern.

Verbs that end in **-uir** add a _____ before all conjugated forms

except _____ .

10.38 Now write these equivalents.

huir	**construir**	**destruir**
run away	*build*	*destroy*

_____   _____   _____

We run away.   *Do you build houses?*   *They destroy the building.*

_____   _____   _____

I don't run away.   *We build bridges.*   *He doesn't destroy anything.*

Look at one more important verb: **oír.**

Oigo un ruido extraño.   Lo oímos.
I hear a strange noise.   *We hear it.*

¿Lo oyes?   ¿Lo oyen ustedes?
Do you hear it?   *Do you all hear it?*

Miguel lo oye.   Ellos dicen que no lo oyen.
Miguel hears it.   *They say they don't hear it.*

10.39 Fill in the blanks.

oír means _____ . It is conjugated like **-uir** verbs, except in

the _____ form, which is _____ .

10.40 Answer the following questions.

¿Qué oyes en la mañana?

¿Oye bien tu mejor amigo?

Cuando practicas español, ¿quiénes oyen?

To Ask People Where They Go to Do Certain Things

First, let's look at the verb **ir**.

Voy a la ciudad.
I go to the city.

Vamos al campo.
We go to the country.

Vas a los conciertos.
You go to the concerts.

Van al cine.
You all go to the movies.

Va a su casa por la tarde.
She goes home in the afternoon.

Van al trabajo temprano.
They go to work early.

How can you conjugate **ir**? If you take off the ending, there's nothing left! You might say, at least in **el tiempo presente**, that what you have left is an **-ar** verb with an old-fashioned **yo** form. Do you remember the other **yo** forms that end this way?

10.41 Write other similar **yo** forms here.

_____   _____

I am (smart).   *I am (here).*

You also remember several ways of using **dónde**.

Origin: ¿De dónde es Jorge?   Es de México.
                           Where is Jorge from?   *He's from Mexico.*

Location of an event: ¿Dónde es la fiesta?   Es en mi casa.
                           Where is the party?   *It's at my house.*

Location of a person: ¿Dónde está Jorge?   Está en México.
                           Where is Jorge?   *He's in Mexico.*

Location of a place: ¿Dónde está tu casa?   Está en el centro.
                           Where is your house?   *It's downtown.*

Location of a thing: ¿Dónde está mi coche?   Está en el garage.
                           Where is my car?   *It's in the garage.*

Now observe these sentences.

¿Adónde va usted los sábados?
Where do you go on Saturdays?

Voy a la ciudad.
I go to the city.

¿Adónde va su esposa?
Where does your wife go?

Va al mercado.
She goes to the market.

¿Adónde van ustedes los viernes?
Where do you all go on Fridays?

Vamos a casa.
We go home.

¿Adónde van sus hijos?
Where do your children go?

Van al colegio.
They go to school.

No van a ninguna parte.
They don't go anywhere.

10.42 Fill in the blanks.

In Spanish, the verb **ir** is followed by _____ , to indicate movement *toward*

a destination. To ask someone's destination, the question word is _____ . If

the destination is *nowhere*, say _____ .

Quick Tip

To indicate where someone is leaving from, use *de.* For example:

Susana va de su casa al mercado.
Susana goes from her house to the market.

Luego va del mercado a su casa.
Then she goes from the market to her house.

10.43 Answer these questions.

¿Adónde vas los sábados por la noche?

¿Adónde va tu amigo los domingos?

¿Van tú y tus amigos a la playa con frecuencia?

¿Cuándo van tus vecinos a tu casa?

¿Con qué frecuencia vas a la casa de tus vecinos?

10.44 Write a question for each of the following answers.

Voy a mi casa.

Vamos los viernes.

No, no va conmigo.

Van a la playa.

Quick Tip

When *a* occurs before *el*, it is always contracted to *al.*

It's a Wrap

You have learned a lot in this chapter. The best way to remember all this is to keep practicing. Talk to yourself and to others. Practice asking and answering **¿Qué hace?** **¿Con quién . . . ? ¿Cuándo . . . ? ¿A qué hora . . . ? ¿Dónde . . . ? ¿Con qué frecuencia . . . ?** Use the verbs that represent the activities that are most important to you. Keep up the good work!

Telling About Actions Toward Oneself, Other People, and Objects

Do I Need to Read This Chapter?

➡️ Do I know how to use a verb that has **se** attached to its infinitive form?

➡️ Do I know how to express the concepts of *self* and *each other*?

➡️ Do I know how to express *him, her, it, us, you,* and *them* in Spanish?

Some of the Verbs I Want to Use Have *se* Attached to Their Infinitives in the Dictionary

Quite a few Spanish verbs are like this. It means that they must always be used with a reflexive pronoun; otherwise they have either a different meaning or no meaning at all.

Get Started

To get a feel for using verbs like this, read, listen to, and memorize the following dialogue.

Dialogue 19   *De vacaciones*

Ligia	Inés
Oye, amiga, ¿qué haces tú para relajarte cuando te quedas en la ciudad durante las vacaciones? *Listen, what do you do to relax when you stay home during your vacation?*	Pues, en primer lugar, me despierto naturalmente, sin despertador. *Well, first, I wake up naturally, without an alarm clock.*
Sí, ¿y después? *And then?*	Me quedo en la cama como media hora, luego me levanto y hago unos ejercicios. *I stay in bed about a half hour, then I get up and do a few exercises.*
Entonces, no tienes prisa para nada. *Then you're not in a hurry to do anything.*	Exactamente. Bajo a la cocina, me preparo un café y leo el periódico. *Exactly. I go down to the kitchen, make myself a cup of coffee, and read the newspaper.*
¿Siempre desayunas antes de vestirte? *Do you always have breakfast before you get dressed?*	Durante las vacaciones, sí. Me baño, me lavo los dientes, me visto, me maquillo y finalmente estoy lista para salir. *During my vacation, yes. I take a bath, brush my teeth, get dressed, put on my makeup, and then I'm ready to go out.*

Ligia	Inés
¿Adónde vas? *Where do you go?*	Depende. Voy a algún museo o de compras o a visitar a una amiga. Siempre me divierto. *It depends. I go to a museum or shopping or to visit a friend. I always have fun.*
¿No te aburres nunca? *Don't you ever get bored?*	Claro que no me aburro. En las tardes me siento en el sofá y leo una novela. Y cuando leo, siempre me duermo. *Of course I don't get bored. In the afternoon I sit on the sofa and read a novel. And I always fall asleep when I read.*
¡Qué divino! Pero ¿no te cansas de estar sola? *Fantastic! But don't you get tired of being alone?*	Ay, no. Todas las noches salgo a bailar con un grupo de amigos. Nos quedamos en un club hasta muy tarde, nos reímos mucho y la pasamos muy bien. La verdad, no me quejo de nada. *No way. I go out dancing every night with a group of friends. We stay at a club until late, we laugh a lot, and we have a good time. Really, I have no complaints.*

Observe these verbs.

	levantarse *get up*	perderse (ie) *get lost*	divertirse (ie) *have a good time*
(yo)	me levanto	me pierdo	me divierto
(tú)	te levantas	te pierdes	te diviertes
(Ud./él/ella)	se levanta	se pierde	se divierte
(Uds./ellos/as)	se levantan	se pierden	se divierten
(nosotros/as)	nos levantamos	nos perdemos	nos divertimos

Test Yourself

11.1 Now write the pattern.

When the infinitive has **se** attached, the conjugated forms are preceded by the following:

_____ before the form that ends in **-o**

_____ before the form that ends in **-as** or **-es**

_____ before the forms that end in **-a/-e/-an/-en**

_____ before the forms that end in **-mos**

Here are some common verbs of this type.

-ar		-er	-ir
acostarse (ue) *lie down*	lavarse la cara *wash one's face*	ponerse la ropa *put on one's clothes*	aburrirse *get bored*
afeitarse *shave*	lavarse los dientes *brush one's teeth*	volverse (ue) loco/a *go crazy*	dormirse (ue) *fall asleep*
cansarse *get tired*	lavarse las manos *wash one's hands*		reírse (i) *laugh*
bañarse *take a bath*	maquillarse *put makeup on*		reunirse *get together*
despertarse (ie) *wake up*	peinarse *comb one's hair*		sentirse (ie) *feel*
enamorarse *fall in love*	quedarse *stay*		vestirse (i) *get dressed*
enojarse *get mad*	quejarse *complain*		irse *leave, go away*
desesperarse *lose hope*	quitarse la ropa *take off one's clothes*		
llamarse *be called* (*named*)	sentarse (ie) *sit down*		

Don't Forget

The subject of the sentence is at the end of the verb.

Me   visto

reflexive pronoun   verb/subject

11.2 Write the equivalents.

_____   _____   _____

I wake up.   *You get dressed.*   *He brushes his teeth.*

_____	_____	_____
She complains.	*We feel.*	*We sit down.*
_____	_____	_____
They stay.	*He shaves.*	*She puts on makeup.*
_____	_____	_____
They don't comb their hair.	*I wash my face.*	*He washes his hands.*
_____	_____	_____
I take a bath.	*He takes off his shoes.*	*We laugh.*
_____	_____	_____
They have a good time.	*She goes crazy.*	*Do you get bored?*
_____	_____	_____
They get tired.	*He gets up.*	*He puts on his hat.*
_____	_____	_____
I get mad.	*They fall in love.*	*She loses hope.*

Don't Forget

Review the parts of the body (p. 53) to use with *lavarse.* For example, wash one's hair = *lavarse el pelo.* Review the nouns that represent articles of clothing (pp. 73-74) to use with *ponerse* and *quitarse.* For example, take off one's coat = *quitarse el abrigo.*

Write five sentences using these verbs to answer the question.

¿Qué haces todos los días?

11.3 Make questions for the following answers.

Se despierta a las seis de la mañana.

Sí, nos quejamos.

No, no se enojan.

Me siento bien.

Look at the verb **llamarse,** a verb used to ask the name of a person or thing. It is very common to use **¿Cómo se llama?** as an alternative to **¿Cuál es su nombre?** To answer this question, you can use the same verb.

Me llamo Sergio.
I'm called Sergio.

Nos llamamos María y Sergio.
We're called Maria and Sergio.

¿Te llamas Gustavo?
Are you called Gustavo?

¿Se llaman Gustavo y Esteban?
Are you all called Gustavo and Esteban?

Se llama Margarita.
She's called Margarita.

Se llaman Margarita y Luisa.
They're called Margarita and Luisa.

11.4 Follow the first example to complete the chart.

¿Cuál es su nombre?
What's your name?

Mi nombre es Bárbara López.
My name is Barbara Lopez.

¿Cómo se llama usted?
What are you called?

Me llamo Bárbara López.
I'm called Barbara Lopez.

_____
What's his name?

_____
His name is Jose.

_____
What is he called?

_____
He's called Jose.

_____
What is her name?

_____
Her name is Juanita.

_____
What is she called?

_____
She's called Juanita.

_____
What are your friends' names?

_____
Their names are Miguel and Juan.

_____
What are your friends called?

_____
My friends are called Miguel and Juan.

11.5 Practice answering the following questions in complete sentences; then listen to them on the recording, pausing it to answer them again. After you have given your answer, a speaker will give his own personal answer, which will probably not be exactly like yours. Other acceptable answers are given in the Answer Key in the Appendix.

¿Cómo te llamas?

¿Cómo se llama tu mejor amigo?

¿Cómo se llaman tus vecinos?

¿Cómo se llama la ciudad donde vives?

I Thought Reflexive Pronouns Meant *Self*

They can—but as we saw in the previous examples, they usually don't translate that way into English.

Observe and compare the following.

La madre se viste.	La madre viste al niño.
The mother gets dressed.	*The mother dresses the child.*
El padre se peina.	El padre peina a la niña.
The father combs his hair.	*The father combs the child's hair.*
Me despierto.	Despierto a mis hijos.
I wake up.	*I wake my children up.*
El chico se pierde.	El chico pierde el libro.
The boy gets lost.	*The boy loses the book.*
Ana se corta el pelo.	Ana corta la torta.
Ana cuts her hair.	*Ana cuts the cake.*
Mi amigo se llama Juan.	Mi amigo llama a su madre.
My friend is called Juan.	*My friend calls his mother.*

Here are some examples that *do* translate as *self* in English.

Me miro en el espejo.	Miro al muchacho.
I look at myself in the mirror.	*I look at the boy.*
Te lastimas.	Lastimas a tus amigos.
You hurt yourself.	*You hurt your friends.*
Ella se sirve.	Ella les sirve a los otros.
She serves herself.	*She serves the others.*
Pedro se ayuda.	Pedro ayuda a su hermano.
Pedro helps himself.	*Pedro helps his brother.*

A funny thing happens in the plural—these have double meanings.

Nos miramos.	Nos miramos.
We look at ourselves.	*We look at each other.*
Nos hablamos.	Nos hablamos.
We talk to ourselves.	*We talk to each other.*

(Ustedes) se lastiman.	(Ustedes) se lastiman.
You all hurt yourselves.	*You all hurt each other.*
Se sirven.	Se sirven.
They serve themselves.	*They serve each other.*
Se cuidan.	Se cuidan.
They take care of themselves.	*They take care of each other.*

11.6 Complete the following.

_____   _____   _____
I help myself.   *She serves herself.*   *We talk to each other.*

_____   _____   _____
They call each other.   *Do you take care of yourself?*   *Do you all help each other?*

11.7 Practice answering the following questions in complete sentences; then listen to them on the recording, pausing it to answer them again. After you have given your answer, a speaker will give his own personal answer, which will probably not be exactly like yours. Other acceptable answers are given in the Answer Key in the Appendix.

¿Se hablan por teléfono tú y tus amigos?

¿Con qué frecuencia se reúnen tú y tus familiares?

¿Cuándo te miras en el espejo?

¿Quién se sirve en tu casa?

¿A qué hora te levantas por la mañana?

¿A qué hora se acuestan las personas con quienes vives?

It's a Wrap

Be sure to look up any of your favorite activities that are not listed here. If the infinitives have **se** attached, add them to this category. Keep practicing—with yourself and with your friends. **¿Te diviertes con el español?**

Talking About Actions Toward Other People and Things

Get Started

Read and listen to the following dialogue, then learn it by heart.

Dialogue 20

Cristina, tu novio habla español muy bien. ¿Te ayuda con tu tarea? *Cristina, your boyfriend speaks Spanish very well. Does he help you with your homework?*	Sí, me ayuda con mi tarea. La lee, pero no la corrige. Me dice si hay errores, y yo los corrijo. *Yes, he helps me with my homework. He reads it but he doesn't correct it. He tells me if there are any mistakes, and I correct them.*
¡Qué bueno! Así aprendes más, ¿verdad? *That's great! You learn more that way, don't you?*	Claro. Además, cuando me llama por teléfono, nos hablamos en español. *Yes. Also, when he calls me on the phone, we talk to each other in Spanish.*
¿Lo ves todos los días? *Do you see him every day?*	No. No lo veo entre semana, sólo los fines de semana. *No, I don't see him on weekdays, only on weekends.*
¿Lo llamas a veces? *Do you ever call him?*	Si necesito algo, lo llamo. Pero por lo general él me llama a mí. *If I need something, I call him. But he usually calls me.*
¿Siempre llevas tu celular contigo? *Do you always carry your cell phone?*	Sí, lo tengo aquí en mi cartera. *Yes, I have it here in my handbag.*

Observe the following sentences.

Jaime mira <u>el periódico</u>. *Jaime looks at the newspaper.*	Jaime mira a <u>su amigo</u>. *Jaime looks at his friend.*
Marta visita <u>el museo</u>. *Marta visits the museum.*	Marta visita a <u>Carlos</u>. *Marta visits Carlos.*
Sara y yo queremos <u>chocolate</u>. *Sara and I want chocolate.*	Sara y yo queremos a <u>nuestra mamá</u>. *Sara and I love our mother.*
Tomás y Miguel necesitan <u>dinero</u>. *Tomas and Miguel need money.*	Tomás y Miguel necesitan a <u>sus padres</u>. *Tomas and Miguel need their parents.*
Raquel prefiere <u>el vestido rojo</u>. *Raquel prefers the red dress.*	Raquel prefiere al <u>profesor exigente</u>. *Raquel prefers the strict teacher.*
Ramón escucha <u>la música</u>. *Ramon listens to the music.*	Ramón escucha a <u>la profesora</u>. *Ramon listens to the teacher.*
Extraño <u>mi país</u>. *I miss my country.*	Extraño a <u>mi novio</u>. *I miss my boyfriend.*

11.8 Fill in the blanks.

The underlined words in the above sentences are <u>direct objects</u>. Spanish signals that the direct object is a person or people by putting _____ before it.

The verb **querer** means _____ when it refers to a *thing;* it means _____ when it refers to a *person.*

Don't Forget

When *a* occurs before *el*, it is always contracted to *al.*

11.9 Write in the equivalents.

_____ *I want a car.*	_____ *I love my friend.*	_____ *We visit the school.*
_____ *We visit the teachers.*	_____ *She looks at the building.*	_____ *She looks at the students.*
_____ *He listens to the radio.*	_____ *He doesn't listen to his mother.*	_____ *Do you call your boyfriend?*

Compare the following.

Quiero la bicicleta.	Quiero a Carolina.
I want the bicycle.	*I love Carolina.*
La quiero.	La quiero.
I want it.	*I love her.*
Visitamos el museo.	Visitamos al director.
We visit the museum.	*We visit the director.*
Lo visitamos.	Lo visitamos.
We visit it.	*We visit him.*
Manuel ve los videos.	Manuel ve a los estudiantes.
Manuel watches the videos.	*Manuel sees the students.*
Manuel los ve.	Manuel los ve.
He watches them.	*Manuel sees them.*
Escuchan las canciones.	Escuchan a Lupe y a Paquita.
They listen to the songs.	*They listen to Lupe and Paquita.*
Las escuchan.	Las escuchan.
They listen to them.	*They listen to them.*

11.10　Fill in the blanks.

Lo can mean ＿＿＿＿＿ or ＿＿＿＿＿ ; **la** can mean ＿＿＿＿＿ or ＿＿＿＿＿ ; **los** means ＿＿＿＿＿ ; **las** means ＿＿＿＿＿ . These direct object pronouns are placed ＿＿＿＿＿ the conjugated verb.

11.11　Rewrite the sentences, changing the <u>underlined words</u> to direct object pronouns.

No queremos <u>el chocolate</u>.　＿＿＿＿＿＿＿＿＿＿＿＿＿＿＿＿ .

Escucho a <u>mis profesores</u>.　＿＿＿＿＿＿＿＿＿＿＿＿＿＿＿＿ .

María ve <u>la televisión</u>.　＿＿＿＿＿＿＿＿＿＿＿＿＿＿＿＿ .

Quiere mucho a <u>su papá</u>.　＿＿＿＿＿＿＿＿＿＿＿＿＿＿＿＿ .

Quiere <u>el coche</u>.   _____ .

El hombre extraña a <u>su novia</u>.   _____ .

Don't Forget

The subject of the sentence is at the end of the verb.

verb/subject   direct object   direct object   verb/subject

Escuchamos la música.   La escuchamos.
We listen to the music.   *We listen to it.*

To Express *me, you,* and *us*

Observe the following sentences.

Juan me llama.	Juan me visita.	Juan me ayuda.
Juan calls me.	*Juan visits me.*	*Juan helps me.*
Yo te llamo.	Te visito.	Te ayudo.
I call you.	*I visit you.*	*I help you.*
Yo lo llamo.	Lo visito.	Lo ayudo.
Yo la llamo.	La visito.	La ayudo.
I call you. (**usted**)	*I visit you.* (**usted**)	*I help you.* (**usted**)
Yo los llamo.	Los visito.	Los ayudo.
Yo las llamo.	Las visito.	Las ayudo.
I call you all.	*I visit you all.*	*I help you all.*
María nos llama.	Nos visita.	Nos ayuda.
Maria calls us.	*She visits us.*	*She helps us.*

11.12 Fill in the blanks with direct object pronouns.

me = _____

you = _____ (a good friend)

you = _____ (a formal acquaintance who is male)

you = _____ (a formal acquaintance who is female)

you all = _____ (several people, all male or a mixed group)

you all = _____ (several people, all female)

us = _____

11.13 Write the equivalents.

_____	_____	_____
She helps me.	*He picks me up.*	*They call me.*
_____	_____	_____
They choose you.	*He loves you.*	*We help you.*
_____	_____	_____
I listen to you all.	*I love you all.*	*He visits you all.*
_____	_____	_____
I love you.	*Do you love me?*	*I miss you.*
_____	_____	_____
They miss us.	*He calls us.*	*Do you listen to us?*

Observe the following questions and answers.

¿Quién te ayuda?   Mi madre me ayuda.
Who helps you?   *My mother helps me.*

¿A quién ayudas?   Ayudo a mi hermano.
Who do you help?   *I help my brother.*

11.14 Write the equivalents.

_____	_____
Who do you call?	*Who calls you?*
_____	_____
I call my father.	*My father calls me.*
_____	_____
Who do they visit?	*Who visits them?*
_____	_____
They visit their grandmother.	*Their grandmother visits them.*

11.15 Practice answering the following questions in complete sentences; then listen to them on the recording, pausing it to answer them again. After you have given your answer, a speaker will give his own personal answer, which will probably not be exactly like yours. Other acceptable answers are given in the Answer Key in the Appendix.

 ¿Quién te llama por teléfono?

¿A quién llamas?

¿Quién visita a tu mejor amigo?

¿A quién visita tu amigo?

¿Quién te quiere?

¿A quién quieres?

11.16 Make up questions for the following answers.

Sí, los extraño mucho.

Lo llamo todos los dias.

Sí, lo estudio.

No, no lo estudian.

Sí, te quiero mucho.

Talk to yourself about the things you see and use every day, the people you see, call, and visit, and those who see, call, and visit you. Think in Spanish about the people you love and those who love you. Make direct objects fun!

◆◆◆◆◆◆◆◆◆◆◆◆◆◆◆◆◆◆◆◆◆◆◆◆◆◆◆◆◆◆◆◆◆◆

CHAPTER 12

Telling About Interactions and Feelings

◆◆◆◆◆◆◆◆◆◆◆◆◆◆◆◆◆◆◆◆◆◆◆◆◆◆◆◆◆◆◆◆◆◆

Do I Need to Read This Chapter?

➡ Can I express interactions like *giving, showing,* and *telling*?

➡ Can I explain in Spanish what I like and don't like, what I love, what fascinates me, and what drives me crazy?

How Are *Giving, Showing,* and *Telling* Different from Other Verbs?

These three verbs—among others—represent an exchange of something between two or more people: the first person (the subject) passes something (the direct object) to the second person (the indirect object). The verb chosen defines the way the thing is passed. Spanish has a special pattern for using these verbs.

Get Started

Read, listen to, and learn the dialogue using the usual steps.

Dialogue 21   Regalos.

¿Cómo celebran ustedes los cumpleaños en tu familia? ¿Se dan regalos? *How do you all celebrate birthdays in your family? Do you give each other presents?*	Pues, por lo general, sí, pero no es nada obligatorio. Depende de muchas cosas. *Yeah, usually, but it's not really necessary. It depends on a lot of things.*
¿Qué le das a tu hermana, por ejemplo? *What do you give your sister, for example?*	A mi hermana le regalo algo cómico, como un libro de chistes o algo por el estilo. *I give her something funny, like a book of jokes or something like that.*
Y a tu papá, ¿qué le regalas? *And what do you give your dad?*	Pues, a mi papá le compro quizás una camisa de colores brillantes, porque se viste demasiado conservador. *Oh, I might give my dad a loud shirt because he dresses way too conservatively.*
Entonces, ¿todos tus regalos son chistosos? *So all your presents are funny?*	Realmente, no. A mi mamá siempre le mando rosas rojas y la invito a cenar a un restaurante elegante. *Not really. I always send my mother red roses and I take her out to a fancy restaurant for dinner.*

¿De veras? ¿Cómo es posible con lo poco que ganas?
Really? How can you do that on the little you earn?
A ti, ¿qué te regalan?
What do they give you?

Pues, le pido el dinero a mi papá.
No problem, I ask my dad for the money.

Mi hermana me da algo cómico, mi papá me compra ropa muy conservadora y mi mamá siempre me prepara una comida muy rica y un pastel especial.
My sister gives me something funny, my dad gives me conservative clothes, and my mother always makes me a delicious dinner and a special cake.

Observe the following sentences.

Le <u>doy</u> mi libro a mi hermana.
I give my book to my sister.

Le <u>das</u> el informe al jefe.
You give the report to the boss.

El jefe me <u>da</u> dinero a mí.
The boss gives me money.

Le <u>damos</u> gracias a nuestro padre.
We give thanks to our father.

Le <u>dan</u> el informe al jefe.
You all give the report to the boss.

Los profesores me <u>dan</u> consejos a mí.
The teachers give me advice.

Test Yourself

12.1 Fill in the blanks.

The verb **dar** is conjugated just like other _____ verbs, except for the slightly different _____ form, which is _____ .

Now look at these sentences.

El jefe   me da el dinero a mí.
The boss   gives me the money.

te da el dinero a ti.
gives you the money.

le da el dinero a usted.
gives you the money.

le da el dinero a Juan. / le da el dinero a él.
gives Juan the money. / gives him the money.

le da el dinero a Sara. / le da el dinero a ella.
gives Sara the money. / gives her the money.

nos da el dinero a nosotros. / a nosotras.
gives the money to us.

les da el dinero a ustedes.
gives the money to you all.

les da el dinero a ellos. / a ellas.
gives the money to them.

12.2 Complete the following.

a + pronoun or name	indirect object pronoun	**a** + pronoun or name	indirect object pronoun
a mí *to me*	me *me*	_____ *to us*	_____ *us*
_____ *to you (**tú**)*	_____ *you (**tú**)*	_____ *to you all*	_____ *you all*
_____ *to you (**usted**)*	_____ *you (**usted**)*		
_____ *to him*	_____ *him*	_____ *to them (males)*	_____ *them*
_____ *to Juan*	_____ *him*	_____ *to Juan and Carlos*	_____ *them*
_____ *to her*	_____ *her*	_____ *to them (females)*	_____ *them*
_____ *to my mother*	_____ *her*	_____ *to my mother and sister*	_____ *them*

Let's analyze a typical sentence.

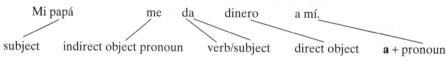

Mi papá	me	da	dinero	a mí.
subject	indirect object pronoun	verb/subject	direct object	**a** + pronoun

The subject and the **a** + pronoun can change positions.

A mí   me   da   dinero   mi papá.

The subject can be omitted (because it is also included in the verb).

A mí   me   da   dinero.

The **a** + pronoun can be omitted. (It only emphasizes the receiver.)

Me   da   dinero.

Observe another sentence.

Mis padres   le   dan   un coche   a mi hermano.

subject   indirect object pronoun   verb/subject   direct object   **a** + noun

A mi hermano   le   dan   un coche   mis padres.

A mi hermano   le   dan   un coche.

A él   le   dan   un coche.

Le dan un coche.

12.3 Now do the same with this sentence. First, indicate the parts of speech.

Elena y yo   le   damos   los libros   a Ana.

_____   _____   _____   _____   _____

Move the **a** + noun to the beginning and the subject to the end.

_____

Omit the subject.

_____

Omit the **a** + noun.

_____

12.4 Now write the pattern.

With exchange verbs, an _____ must precede the conjugated verb. The _____ and the _____ are optional.

Observe the following.

Correct: El jefe me da dinero a mí. El jefe me da dinero.
Incorrect: ~~El jefe da dinero a mí.~~
Correct: El jefe le da dinero a Juan. El jefe le da dinero.
Incorrect: ~~El jefe da dinero a Juan.~~

12.5 Now write the pattern.

When there is an exchange of something between two or more people, the person who is the receiver may be identified two ways:

a + pronoun, noun, or name <u>and</u> an indirect object pronoun

If only one of these ways is given, it must be the _____ .

12.6 Complete the following, using the pattern in the example.

Mi mamá me da dinero a mí.   Enrique le da dulces a ella.
Mi mamá me da dinero.   Enrique le da dulces
She gives me money.   *He gives her candy.*

_____   _____

_____   _____
I give him the books.   *Maria gives you the magazines.*

_____   _____

_____   _____
We give you the car.   *His cousins give him work.*

_____   _____

_____   _____
Do you give her money?   *Do your friends give you candy?*

_____   _____

_____   _____
The boss gives them an opportunity.   *The boss doesn't give us anything.*

12.7 Answer these questions.

¿A quién le das dinero?

¿Quién te da dinero a ti?

¿Le das algo a tu mejor amigo?

¿Tu mejor amigo te da algo?

Here are more verbs that indicate exchanges of something from one person to another.

comprar *buy for*	devolver (ue) *return (something) to*	decir (i) (digo) *tell to*
enseñar *teach to*	prometer *promise to*	escribir *write to*

enviar *send to*	pedir (i) *ask for*
explicar *explain to*	
mandar *send to*	
mostrar (ue) *show to*	
preguntar *ask (of)*	
preparar *prepare for*	
prestar *lend to*	
regalar *give as a gift to*	
asegurar *assure*	

12.8 Complete the following.

_____ *She shows the photos to me.*	_____ *He sends her letters.*	_____ *We return the gifts to them.*
_____ *I tell her my secrets.*	_____ *They write us letters.*	_____ *He prepares dinner for her.*
_____ *He sends me email.*	_____ *They buy her flowers.*	_____ *She explains math to me.*

12.9 Practice answering the following questions in complete sentences; then listen to them on the recording, pausing it to answer them again. After you have given your answer, a speaker will give his own personal answer, which will probably not be exactly like yours. Other acceptable answers are given in the Answer Key in the Appendix.

¿Quién te dice sus secretos?

¿A quién le dices tus ideas más fantásticas?

¿Quiénes te escriben email?

¿A quiénes les escribes email?

12.10 Write a question for each of the following answers.

Les mando tarjetas a mis abuelos.

Mis amigos me muestran sus fotos.

Mi mamá me prepara la cena.

Le escribo cartas de amor a mi novio.

Mis amigos me prestan dinero.

To Express Asking a Question and Asking for Something

Use the exchange-verb pattern—but bear in mind that these two actions are represented by two different verbs in Spanish. Observe the following examples.

Le   pregunto   a María   dónde vive

indirect object   verb/subject   **a** + name   direct object

Le pregunto a María adónde va.
I ask Maria where she is going.

María me contesta que va al cine.
Maria answers that she's going to the movies.

Le pregunto a María qué hace.
I ask Maria what she does.

María me contesta que estudia mucho.
Maria answers that she studies a lot.

Le pregunto a María si ve la tele.
I ask Maria if she watches TV.

María me contesta que sí.
Maria answers yes.

María me pregunta si veo la tele.
Maria asks me if I watch TV.

Le contesto que no.
I answer no.

12.11 Fill in the blanks.

To ask a question, use the verb _____ . Identify the person who is being asked with an _____ .

The "thing being exchanged" is a whole phrase—the question.

If it's a yes-or-no question, use _____ before the verb.

Now look at the verb used for making a request: **pedir (i).**

Le pido dinero a María.
I ask Maria for money.

Le pedimos dinero a María.
We ask Maria for money.

Le pides los billetes a Cristina.
You ask Cristina for the tickets.

Le piden los billetes a Cristina.
You all ask Cristina for the tickets.

María le pide la información a Raúl.   Le piden la información a Raúl.
Maria asks Raul for the information.   *They ask Raul for the information.*

12.12 Fill in the blanks.

To *ask for* something, use the verb _____ . Identify the person who is being asked with an _____ .

12.13 Complete the following.

_____   _____

I ask Juan for my books.   *I ask Juan if he reads them.*

_____   _____

We ask Juanita where she goes.   *She answers that she goes home.*

_____   _____

The teacher asks us for the homework.   *The teacher asks us where Juan is.*

12.14 Now answer these questions.

¿Qué le preguntas a tu mejor amigo?

¿Qué te contesta?

¿Qué les pides a tus profesores o a tus colegas?

¿Qué hacen ellos?

What If I Get Direct Object and Indirect Object Pronouns Mixed Up?

Because direct and indirect object pronouns are the same in English, this can be confusing at first. Try to think of their functions in Spanish rather than translating from English. To help you get used to using them in the same sentence, read, listen to, and learn the following dialogue.

Dialogue 22 ⊙

Victor	Germán
Oye, Germán, ¿tienes dinero? *Listen, German—do you have any money?*	Y ¿por qué me lo preguntas? *Why do you ask me that?*
Pues, porque salgo con una chica linda esta noche y no tengo dinero para el cine. ¿Me lo prestas? *Um—because I'm going out with a beautiful girl tonight and I don't have enough money for the movies. Will you lend it to me?*	Víctor, tú sabes que yo tampoco tengo mucho, pero, bueno, aquí tienes lo poco que me queda. *Victor, you know I don't have much either, but here's the little I have left.*

Victor	Germán
Eres el mejor hermano del mundo. *You're the best brother in the world.*	Hay una condición . . . *There's one condition . . .*
¿Sí? ¿Cuál es? *Yeah? What's that?*	Preséntame a la chica. *Introduce me to the girl.*
Pero por supuesto, hermano, te la presento esta misma noche. *Of course, I'll introduce her to you tonight.*	Y pregúntale si tiene una hermana tan linda como ella. *And ask her if she has a sister as pretty as she is.*
La llamo ahora mismo y se lo pregunto. *I'll call her right now and I'll ask her.*	Entonces, vamos los cuatro al cine. *Then we can all four go to the movies.*
¿Y el dinero? *What about the money?*	Pues, se lo pedimos a mi papá. *We'll ask Dad for it.*

Observe the following examples.

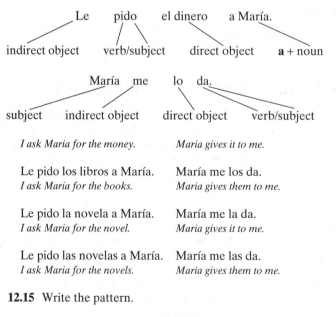

Le   pido   el dinero   a María.

indirect object   verb/subject   direct object   **a** + noun

María   me   lo   da.

subject   indirect object   direct object   verb/subject

I ask Maria for the money.	*Maria gives it to me.*
Le pido los libros a María. *I ask Maria for the books.*	María me los da. *Maria gives them to me.*
Le pido la novela a María. *I ask Maria for the novel.*	María me la da. *Maria gives it to me.*
Le pido las novelas a María. *I ask Maria for the novels.*	María me las da. *Maria gives them to me.*

12.15 Write the pattern.

When the indirect and direct objects are stated in pronouns, these pronouns are positioned _____ the verb. If both objects are in pronoun form, the _____ goes before the _____ .

12.16 Write the equivalents.

I ask my father for the car.	*My father gives it to me.*
We ask our sister for the recipe.	*She gives it to us.*
You ask me for the books.	*I give them to you.*
I ask my brother for the keys.	*He gives them to me.*

Now observe the following sentences.

Isabel me pide el coche. *Isabel asks me for the car.*	Le doy el coche. *I give her the car.*	Se lo doy. *I give it to her.*
Usted me pide los libros. *You ask me for the books.*	Le doy los libros. *I give you the books.*	Se los doy. *I give them to you.*
Nuestra hermana nos pide la receta. *Our sister asks us for the recipe.*	Le damos la receta. *We give her the recipe.*	Se la damos. *We give it to her.*
Mi hermano me pide las llaves. *My brother asks me for the keys.*	Le doy las llaves. *I give him the keys.*	Se las doy. *I give them to him.*

12.17 Write the pattern.

When the indirect object pronoun is **le** or **les,** it changes to _____ when it occurs before a direct object pronoun.

12.18 Write the following equivalents.

The teacher asks us for the composition.	*We give it to her.*
My friend asks me for a newspaper.	*I give it to him.*
Ana and Berta ask Juan for the car.	*He gives it to them.*
They ask him for the keys.	*He gives them to them.*

12.19   Answer the following questions.

¿Tu mejor amigo te dice   ¿Cuándo te las dice?
    sus ideas?

¿Le dices tus secretos a   ¿Cuándo se los dices?
    tu mejor amigo?

12.20   Make questions for the following answers.

Sí, se lo doy.   Sí, nos lo dice.

No, no me la presta.   Sí, se lo manda.

Let's Compare the Object Pronouns

Observe the following chart.

Reflexive Pronouns used with verbs that have *se* attached to the infinitive form		Direct Object Pronouns used to complete the action of the verb		Indirect Object Pronouns used to indicate the person who receives something from someone else	
me *ø*/myself	nos *ø/ourselves* *each other*	me *me*	nos *us*	me *me*	nos *us*
te *ø*/yourself	se *ø/yourselves* *each other*	te *you*	los/las *you all*	te *you*	les/se[†] *you all*
se *ø*/yourself *ø*/himself *ø*/herself	se *ø/yourselves* *ø/themselves* *each other*	lo/la *him/her/it*	los/las *them*	le/se[†] *you* *him/her*	les/se[†] *you all* *them*

*ø means that there is no direct equivalent for this form in English. See Chapter 11.
[†]Only before **lo/la/los/las**.

Don't Forget

The best way to learn these patterns is to practice saying model sentences in Spanish. Translating from English is what makes them confusing.

Talk to yourself—aloud, of course—about who you give, show, or tell things to, what you give them, and when. Then talk about who gives, shows, and tells things to you. Keep practicing! **Esto no es imposible. Te lo aseguramos.**

Expressing Feelings

A number of verbs express the cause of personal feelings. These verbs have a special pattern in Spanish.

First, to get a feel for these patterns, read, listen to, and memorize the dialogue.

Dialogue 23

Amigos, ¿qué les gusta hacer durante las vacaciones?
Hey, guys, what do you like to do during your vacation?

Y a ti, Patricia, ¿qué te gusta hacer?
And you, Patricia, what do you like to do?

¿No te fastidia el tráfico?
Doesn't the traffic annoy you?

A ti te interesa más la playa, ¿verdad, Érica?
You're more interested in the beach, right, Erica?

¿Qué haces por la noche?
What do you do at night?

Paco: A mí me gusta pescar, así que voy a un lago en las montañas cada año.
I like to go fishing, so I go to a lake in the mountains every year.

Patricia: Yo no voy a las montañas porque me molestan mucho los mosquitos. Me gustan más las ciudades grandes y los hoteles de lujo.
I don't go to the mountains because the mosquitoes bother me a lot. I like big cities and luxury hotels.

Si estoy de vacaciones, no, porque voy a todos lados en taxi.
When I'm on vacation, no, because I go everywhere by taxi.

Érica: Pues sí, me encanta la playa, porque me gusta broncearme. Además, prefiero el ambiente informal.
Yeah, I love the beach because I like to get a tan, and besides, I prefer the relaxed atmosphere.

Voy a la zona comercial porque me fascinan los juegos que tienen allí.
I go to the commercial area because I love the games they have there.

¿Qué pasa si hace mal tiempo?
What if the weather is lousy?

La verdad no me importa. Me da la oportunidad de leer.
I really don't care. It gives me the chance to read.

Bueno, me parece muy interesante. Creo que el lugar ideal para mí es un país en donde se habla español, porque me fascina la cultura hispana.
Well, this is all very interesting. I think the perfect spot for me is a Spanish-speaking country, because Hispanic culture fascinates me.

Tienes razón, y además, en esos países hay lagos en las montañas, ciudades grandes con hoteles de lujo, playas . . . en fin, hay de todo, y te da la oportunidad de hablar español.
You're right, and besides, in those countries there are mountain lakes, big cities with luxury hotels, beaches—there's everything, plus it gives you the chance to speak Spanish.

Observe the following sentences.

¿Qué te parece la ciudad?
How does the city seem to you?
(*What do you think of the city?*)

Me fascina.
It fascinates me.

Me gusta.
It appeals to me.
(*I like it.*)

Me encanta.
It enchants me.
(*I love it.*)

In each of these examples, the subject—*it*—is expressed at the end of the verb. The indirect object is the person who receives the feeling sent by the subject, and the verb tells what kind of feeling that is. Always think of an indirect object as a person who is *receiving* something—in this case, a feeling.

Quick Tip

With these verbs there is never a direct object. The feeling received is expressed by the verb.

Look at the following example.

        A mí   me   fascina   la ciudad.

a + pronoun   indirect object   verb/subject   subject

The positions of **a mí** and **la ciudad** can be reversed.

La ciudad me fascina a mí.

The **a mí** can be omitted (it only emphasizes *me*).

Me fascina la ciudad.

La ciudad can be omitted (it only emphasizes the verb ending **-a**).

Me fascina.

Quick Tip

Don't try to translate *it.* The verb ending expresses this.

12.21 Write in the equivalents, following the example.

Me gusta el chocolate.   _____   _____
Me gusta.   _____   _____
Chocolate appeals to me.   *The dress appeals to me.*   *The house appeals to me.*
It appeals to me.   *It appeals to me.*   *It appeals to me.*

Quick Tip

While the English expressions *appeal to* and *enchant* are not used often by English-speakers, they will help you understand the patterns used with these verbs.

Look what happens when the subject is plural.

¿Qué te parecen los pueblos pequeños?
How do the small towns seem to you?
(*What do you think of the small towns?*)

Me parecen tranquilos.
They seem quiet to me.
(*I think they're quiet.*)

Me fascinan.
They fascinate me.

Me gustan.
They appeal to me.
(*I like them.*)

Me encantan.
They enchant me.
(*I love them.*)

12.22 Write in the equivalents, following the example.

Me gustan las casas.   _____   _____
Me gustan.   _____   _____
The houses appeal to me.   *The books appeal to me.*   *The cars appeal to me.*
They appeal to me.   *They appeal to me.*   *They appeal to me.*

Quick Tip

Don't translate *they.* The verb endings *-an* and *-en* express this.

In Spanish, it is important to include **el, la, los,** or **las** before a noun subject, even when it has a general meaning.

Observe the following.

Me gustan los libros.
The (specific) books appeal to me. / Books (in general) appeal to me.

Los coches me fascinan.
The cars fascinate me. / Cars fascinate me.

Me encanta el chocolate.
The chocolate enchants me. / Chocolate enchants me.

12.23 Complete the following.

_____   _____
Shoes enchant me.   *These shoes enchant me.*

_____   _____
Mexican food appeals to me.   *The food here appeals to me.*

What If Somebody Else Is the Receiver of the Feeling?

Observe the following sentences.

(A mí) me gusta el chocolate.
Chocolate appeals to me.

(A mí) me gustan los libros.
Books appeal to me.

(A ti) te gusta el chocolate.
Chocolate appeals to you.

(A ti) te gustan los libros.
Books appeal to you.

(A usted) le gusta el chocolate.
Chocolate appeals to you.

(A usted) le gustan los libros.
Books appeal to you.

(A él) le gusta el chocolate.
Chocolate appeals to him.

(A él) le gustan los libros.
Books appeal to him.

(A ella) le gusta el chocolate.
Chocolate appeals to her.

(A ella) le gustan los libros.
Books appeal to her.

(A nosotros) nos gusta el chocolate.
Chocolate appeals to us.

(A nosotros) nos gustan los libros.
Books appeal to us.

(A nosotras) nos gusta el chocolate.
Chocolate appeals to us.

(A nosotras) nos gustan los libros.
Books appeal to us.

(A ustedes) les gusta el chocolate.
Chocolate appeals to you all.

(A ustedes) les gustan los libros.
Books appeal to you all.

(A ellos) les gusta el chocolate.
Chocolate appeals to them.

(A ellos) les gustan los libros.
Books appeal to them.

(A ellas) les gusta el chocolate.
Chocolate appeals to them.

(A ellas) les gustan los libros.
Books appeal to them.

Here are other verbs that follow this pattern.

fastidiar *annoy*	parecer *seem*	aburrir *bore*
importar *be important to*	caer bien *make a good impression*	
interesar *interest*	caer mal *make a bad impression*	
molestar *bother*	volver (ue) loco/a *cause someone to be crazy about / drive someone crazy*	
sacar de quicio *"drive up the wall"*		

Observe these uses of **importar**.

Me importa mi familia.
My family is important to me.

Me importan mis amigos.
My friends are important to me.

No me importa.
It isn't important to me.
I don't care.

Eso no te importa. / ¿Qué te importa?
That isn't important to you.
That's none of your business. / What's it to you?

12.24 Write the equivalents.

_____
The classes fascinate him.

_____
Shoes enchant her.

_____
Novels interest me.

_____
Tacos appeal to us.

_____
The traffic bothers me.

_____
The movie fascinates them.

_____
Are grades important to you?

_____
The class bores us.

_____
Does rock music appeal to you?

To Say That You Like a Person or People

To ask someone's opinion of something or someone, the question is:

¿Qué te parece el chico?   ¿Qué te parecen los chicos?

You can express your first impression of a person or people as follows:

(Él/Ella) me cae bien.
He/She gives me a good impression.

(Ellos) me caen mal.
They give me a bad impression.

Use **gustar** to express that someone attracts you.

(Tú) me gustas.
You attract me.

(Él/Ella) me gusta.
He/She attracts me.

To find out if someone is attracted to you, say:

¿Te gusto?
Do I attract you?

The answer would be:

Sí, me gustas mucho.
Yes, you attract me.

Quick Tips

molestar = bother
abusar = molest

What If Somebody Else Is the Receiver of the Feeling?

Observe the following sentences.

(A mí) me gusta el chocolate.
Chocolate appeals to me.

(A ti) te gusta el chocolate.
Chocolate appeals to you.

(A usted) le gusta el chocolate.
Chocolate appeals to you.

(A él) le gusta el chocolate.
Chocolate appeals to him.

(A ella) le gusta el chocolate.
Chocolate appeals to her.

(A nosotros) nos gusta el chocolate.
Chocolate appeals to us.

(A nosotras) nos gusta el chocolate.
Chocolate appeals to us.

(A ustedes) les gusta el chocolate.
Chocolate appeals to you all.

(A ellos) les gusta el chocolate.
Chocolate appeals to them.

(A ellas) les gusta el chocolate.
Chocolate appeals to them.

(A mí) me gustan los libros.
Books appeal to me.

(A ti) te gustan los libros.
Books appeal to you.

(A usted) le gustan los libros.
Books appeal to you.

(A él) le gustan los libros.
Books appeal to him.

(A ella) le gustan los libros.
Books appeal to her.

(A nosotros) nos gustan los libros.
Books appeal to us.

(A nosotras) nos gustan los libros.
Books appeal to us.

(A ustedes) les gustan los libros.
Books appeal to you all.

(A ellos) les gustan los libros.
Books appeal to them.

(A ellas) les gustan los libros.
Books appeal to them.

Here are other verbs that follow this pattern.

fastidiar	parecer	aburrir
annoy	*seem*	*bore*
importar	caer bien	
be important to	*make a good impression*	
interesar	caer mal	
interest	*make a bad impression*	
molestar	volver (ue) loco/a	
bother	*cause someone to be crazy about / drive someone crazy*	
sacar de quicio		
"drive up the wall"		

Observe these uses of **importar**.

Me importa mi familia.   Me importan mis amigos.
My family is important to me.   *My friends are important to me.*

No me importa.   Eso no te importa. / ¿Qué te importa?
It isn't important to me.   *That isn't important to you.*
I don't care.   *That's none of your business. / What's it to you?*

12.24 Write the equivalents.

_____   _____   _____
The classes fascinate him.   *Shoes enchant her.*   *Novels interest me.*

_____   _____   _____
Tacos appeal to us.   *The traffic bothers me.*   *The movie fascinates them.*

_____   _____   _____
Are grades important to you?   *The class bores us.*   *Does rock music appeal to you?*

To Say That You Like a Person or People

To ask someone's opinion of something or someone, the question is:

¿Qué te parece el chico?   ¿Qué te parecen los chicos?

You can express your first impression of a person or people as follows:

(Él/Ella) me cae bien.   (Ellos) me caen mal.
He/She gives me a good impression.   *They give me a bad impression.*

Use **gustar** to express that someone attracts you.

(Tú) me gustas.
You attract me.

Quick Tips

molestar = bother
abusar = molest

(Él/Ella) me gusta.
He/She attracts me.

To find out if someone is attracted to you, say:

¿Te gusto?
Do I attract you?

The answer would be:

Sí, me gustas mucho.
Yes, you attract me.

To express caring or love for a good friend or a family member, use **querer**.

Te quiero.	¿Me quieres?	Lo quiero.	La quiere.
I care for you.	*Do you care for me?*	*I care for him.*	*He cares for her.*

Use **amar** to express deep, abiding love.

Te amo.	¿Me amas?	Lo amo.	La ama.
I love you.	*Do you love me?*	*I love him.*	*He loves her.*

12.25 Practice answering the following questions in complete sentences; then listen to them on the recording, pausing it to answer them again. After you have given your answer, a speaker will give his own personal answer, which will probably not be exactly like yours. Other acceptable answers are given in the Answer Key in the Appendix.

¿Quién te cae bien?

¿Quién te cae mal?

¿Quién te gusta?

¿A quién le gustas?

¿A quiénes quieres?

¿Quiénes te quieren?

¿Amas a alguien?

¿Alguien te ama?

12.26 Make questions for the following answers.

Sí, me cae muy bien.

Me cae mal.

Sí, le gusta Gustavo.

No, no me molesta.

To Say What Activities You Enjoy

Observe the following sentences.

Me gusta nadar.	Nos fascina bailar.
Swimming appeals to me.	*Dancing fascinates us.*
¿Te gusta cocinar?	¿Les interesa ir a los museos?
Does cooking appeal to you?	*Does going to museums interest you all?*

Le encanta pescar.
Fishing enchants him.

Les aburre ver partidos en la tele.
Watching games on TV bores them.

12.27 Complete the following.

When the subject is an activity, it is expressed in the _____ form of the verb.

12.28 Write the equivalents.

_____

Studying bores him.

_____

Playing football enchants me.

_____

Watching football appeals to me.

_____

Walking appeals to her.

_____

Going to parties fascinates them.

_____

Sleeping appeals to him.

Write four sentences that answer the following questions.

¿Qué te gusta/encanta/molesta/fascina hacer?

It's a Wrap

Practice by asking yourself what pleases, fascinates, annoys, and bothers you. What really drives you up the wall? Then ask your friends the same questions. **¿Te fascina hablar español?**

CHAPTER 13

Describing Activities in Progress

Do I Need to Read This Chapter?

➜ Do I know how to ask people what they're doing right now?

➜ Can I explain that I am in the middle of a project?

➜ Do I know more than one way to say "now"?

How Can *Now* Have More than One Meaning?

When you think about it, "now" is only relative to the period of time you are concentrating on. For example, if you are thinking about your daily activities, "now" is perhaps somewhere between breakfast and lunch, lunch and dinner, or dinner and bedtime. In other words, "this morning," "this afternoon," "this evening," and "tonight" can all mean "now." If you are thinking about your monthly activities, "this week" can mean "now." And so forth and so on.

Let's look at these expressions in Spanish.

ahora			
now			
ahora mismo *right this minute*	estos días *these days*	esta primavera *this spring*	en esta década *during this decade*
en este momento *at the moment*	esta semana *this week*	este verano *this summer*	en este siglo *in this century*
actualmente *currently*	este mes *this month*	este otoño *this fall*	en este milenio *in this millennium*
esta mañana *this morning*	este semestre *this semester*	este invierno *this winter*	ya no *not anymore*
esta tarde *this afternoon*	en esta época *at this time in our lives*	este año *this year*	todavía *still*
esta noche *tonight*			

Get Started

Read and memorize the
following dialogue.

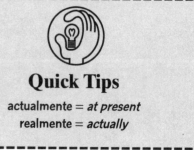

Quick Tips

actualmente = *at present*
realmente = *actually*

Read, listen to, and learn the following dialogue using the usual steps.

Dialogue 24 *Una conversación por teléfono.*

Hola, Martín, soy Alejandro. ¿Qué tal? ¿Qué haces ahora? *Hello, Martin, this is Alejandro. What's up? What are you doing?*	Hola, Alex. Estoy bien, pero un poco ocupado. Fíjate que estoy pintando la sala. *Hi, Alex. I'm fine, but a little busy. Can you believe I'm painting the living room?*
Eso sí es un trabajazo. ¿Lo haces solo o alguien te ayuda? *That's a big job. Are you doing it by yourself, or is someone helping you?*	Lo hago solo. No te imaginas lo aburrido que es. *I'm doing it alone. You can't imagine how boring it is.*
¿Dónde están tus compañeros? ¿Por qué no pintan ellos? *Where are your roommates? Why aren't they painting?*	Bueno, Alberto no está aquí; está estudiando en la biblioteca. Mariano y su novia están arriba viendo la tele, y la verdad no sé dónde está Javier ni qué está haciendo. *Well, Alberto isn't here; he's studying at the library. Mariano and his girlfriend are upstairs watching TV, and I really don't know where Javier is or what he's doing.*
Bueno, yo no estoy haciendo nada. Ahora mismo voy a tu casa para ayudarte. *Well, I'm not doing anything. I'm coming to your house to help you right now.*	Gracias, amigo. Y tráeme un sándwich. Me muero de hambre. *Thanks, friend. And bring me a sandwich. I'm dying of hunger.*

Observe the following sentences.

Pinto la casa ahora. *I'm painting the house.*	Estoy pintando la casa. *I'm painting the house.*
¿Qué comes? *What are you eating?*	¿Qué estás comiendo? *What are you eating?*
Lupe escribe una carta ahora. *Lupe's writing a letter.*	Lupe está escribiendo una carta. *Lupe's writing a letter.*
Estudiamos mucho estos días. *We're studying a lot these days.*	Estamos estudiando mucho estos días. *We're studying a lot these days.*
¿Aprenden mucho este semestre? *Are you all learning a lot this semester?*	¿Están aprendiendo mucho este semestre? *Are you all learning a lot this semester?*
Los niños ya no lloran. *The children aren't crying anymore.*	Los niños ya no están llorando. *The children aren't crying anymore.*

13.1 Fill in the blanks.

To express what is going on at the present time, Spanish has two options: (1) **el tiempo presente** and (2) a conjugated form of the verb _____ followed by another verb that ends in _____ .

Let's Look at the Formation of the -*ndo* Words

These verb forms that end in **-ndo** are called *gerunds*.

Observe the following examples.

-*ar* Verbs	-*er* Verbs	-*ir* Verbs
cocinar: cocinando	aprender: aprendiendo	abrir: abriendo
escuchar: escuchando	comer: comiendo	escribir: escribiendo
hablar: hablando	correr: corriendo	descubrir: descubriendo
preparar: preparando	hacer: haciendo	salir: saliendo

13.2 Now write the patterns.

To form the gerund, take off the _____ , _____ , or _____ from the infinitive of the verb. Add _____ to the stem of **-ar** verbs; add _____ to the stem of **-er** and **-ir** verbs.

13.3 Now write the equivalents.

_____
He is speaking.

_____
We are writing.

_____
They are learning.

_____
Are you listening?

_____
She's running.

_____
I'm preparing.

_____
He's cooking.

_____
We're discovering.

_____
Are they eating?

Look at the following infinitives and gerunds.

leer: leyendo	contribuir: contribuyendo
read	*contribute*
creer: creyendo	distribuir: distribuyendo
believe	*distribute*
caer: cayendo	construir: construyendo
fall	*build*

13.4 Now write the pattern.

To find the stem, first remove the **-er** or **-ir** ending from the infinitive.

If the stem ends in a vowel, add _____ instead of _____ to form the gerund.

Now look at these infinitives and gerunds.

servir (i, i): sirviendo *serve*	mentir (ie, i): mintiendo *lie, make an untrue statement*	dormir (ue, u): durmiendo *sleep*
pedir (i, i): pidiendo *ask for*		morir (ue, u): muriendo *die*
decir (i, i): diciendo *say, tell to*		
vestirse (i, i): vistiéndose *get dressed*		

13.5 Fill in the blanks.

Verbs whose infinitives end in _____ and that indicate vowel changes always have a second vowel-change indication. The second one is used in the _____ form.

13.6 Now write the equivalents.

_____	_____	_____
She's serving the meal.	*They're lying.*	*He's sleeping.*
_____	_____	_____
What are you saying?	*I'm not asking you for money.*	*She's not dying.*

Look at your **Vocabulario personal** and make a note of the **-ir** verbs that indicate vowel changes. Find the second change in your dictionary, and then write out the gerunds of those verbs. Practice using these gerunds out loud so that they will look right and sound right when you come across them.

13.7 Now answer the following questions.

¿Qué estás haciendo ahora?

¿Qué está haciendo tu mejor amigo?

¿Estás aprendiendo francés?

¿Estás haciendo un proyecto esta semana?

¿Tú y tus amigos están trabajando esta semana?

13.8 Make questions for the following answers.

Estamos preparando la cena.

Está trabajando conmigo.

Están viendo una película en la televisión.

No estoy haciendo nada.

How Are Gerunds Used with Reflexive and Object Pronouns?

Observe the following sentences.

- With a reflexive pronoun:

  Me estoy durmiendo.   Estoy durmiéndome.
  I'm falling asleep.   *I'm falling asleep.*

- With a direct object pronoun:

  Está comprando la camisa.
  He's buying the shirt.

  La está comprando.   Está comprándola.
  He's buying it.   *He's buying it.*

- With indirect and direct object pronouns:

  Le está escribiendo una carta.   Está escribiéndole una carta.
  She's writing him a letter.   *She's writing him a letter.*

  Se la está escribiendo.   Está escribiéndosela.
  She's writing it to him.   *She's writing it to him.*

13.9 Write the pattern.

   The reflexive, direct, and indirect object pronouns can be placed either _____
the conjugated form of **estar** or attached to the _____ .

13.10 Write the equivalents, using one of the above patterns.

_____   _____
I'm getting dressed.   *We're getting lost.*

_____   _____
Are you falling asleep?   *Are you all getting tired?*

_____   _____
He's waking up.   *They're falling in love.*

13.11 Write the equivalents, following one of the above patterns.

_____
I'm buying it. (el libro).

_____
We're visiting them. (a los abuelos)

_____
Are you watching it? (el programa)

_____
Are you all selling it? (el coche)

_____
She's calling them. (a sus amigas)

_____
They're looking at us.

13.12 Write the equivalents, following one of the above patterns.

_____
I'm sending it (la carta) *to him.*

_____
We're showing them (las fotos) *to her.*

_____
Are you buying it (el anillo) *for me?*

_____
Are you all teaching it (el baile) *to them?*

_____
He's selling them (los libros) *to me.*

_____
They're explaining it (la lección) *to us.*

Keep practicing these constructions out loud until they feel natural. Make up more examples with the verbs from your **Vocabulario personal.** Ask yourself out loud at different times **¿Qué estoy haciendo? ¡Estás aprendiendo español! ¡Qué bueno!**

Telling How Long an Activity Has Been Going On

Get Started

Read, listen to, and memorize the following dialogue.

Dialogue 25

Rolando, hablas muy bien inglés. ¿Hace cuánto tiempo que vives en este país? *Rolando, you speak English very well. How long have you been living in this country?*	Gracias, Jaime. Hace dos años que vivo aquí, pero llevo unos diez años estudiando inglés. *Thanks, Jaime. I've lived here for two years, but I've been studying English for about ten.*
¿Desde cuándo trabajas en esta empresa? *How long have you worked for this company?*	Estoy trabajando aquí desde junio. Y tú, ¿cúanto tiempo llevas con la empresa? *I've been working here since June. What about you? How long have you worked here?*
Llevo doce años trabajando aquí, y ya me estoy cansando. Creo que es hora de buscar otro trabajo. *I've been working here twelve years, and I'm getting tired. I think it's time to look for another job.*	A lo mejor estás cansado porque te hacen falta unas vacaciones. ¿Por qué no haces un viaje a mi país? *You're probably just tired because you need a vacation. Why don't you take a trip to my country?*
Tienes razón. Llevo dos años sin descansar. ¡Y me encanta la idea de conocer tu país! *You're right. I've had two years without a break. And I love the idea of going to your country.*	Ya te veo más animado. Yo te ayudo con los planes para el viaje. *I see you've cheered up already. I'll help you plan the trip.*

Observe the following sentences.

Hace seis meses que vivo aquí.
I've lived here for six months.

Hace un año que Juan trabaja con nosotros.
Juan has worked with us for a year.

Hace varios meses que estudiamos español.
We've studied Spanish for several months.

13.13 Write the pattern.

To indicate how long an activity has been in progress, use _____ + length of time + _____ + the verb in **el tiempo presente**.

Let's look at some lengths of time.

minutos	semanas	toda la semana	mucho tiempo
minutes	*weeks*	*all week*	*a long time*
horas	meses	todo el mes	siglos
hours	*months*	*all month*	*ages*
días	años	todo el año	toda la vida
days	*years*	*all year*	*one's whole life*

13.14 Now write the equivalents.

_____

I've lived here for five years.

_____

He's worked here for ten years.

_____

We've studied Spanish for several months.

_____

They've been in Mexico for six weeks.

Here is another way to express the same meaning.

Hace seis meses que estoy viviendo aquí.
I've been living here for six months.

Hace un año que Juan está trabajando con nosotros.
Juan has been working with us for a year.

Hace varios meses que estamos estudiando español.
We've been studying Spanish for several months.

13.15 Write the pattern.

To emphasize how long something has been going on, use: _____ + length
of time + _____ + a conjugated form of **estar** + _____

13.16 Answer the following questions.

¿Hace cuánto tiempo que estás viviendo aquí?

¿Hace cuánto tiempo que estás estudiando español?

¿Hace cuánto tiempo que estás haciendo estos ejercicios?

Observe the following sentences.

Llevo seis horas trabajando.
I've been working for six hours.

Llevas mucho tiempo estudiando español.
You've been studying Spanish for a long time.

Mi hermano lleva tres años viviendo en Chile.
My brother has been living in Chile for three years.

Llevamos cinco meses buscando trabajo.
We've been looking for work for five months.

Mis compañeros llevan quince horas leyendo para el examen.
My roommates have been reading for the exam for fifteen hours.

13.17 Write the pattern.

Another way to indicate the length of time an activity has been going on is to use a conjugated form of _____ + length of time + _____ .

13.18 Write the equivalents, using **llevar**.

_____

I've been studying for four years.

_____

She's been looking for work for three months.

_____

We've been watching TV for two hours.

_____

They've been playing tennis for an hour.

To Say Something Hasn't Happened for a Period of Time

Compare the following.

Hace dos años que no estudio.
I haven't studied for two years.

Llevo dos años sin estudiar.
I haven't studied for two years.

Hace cuatro horas que no comes.
You haven't eaten in four hours.

Llevas cuatro horas sin comer.
You haven't eaten in four hours.

Hace un mes que no ve a su novia.
He hasn't seen his girlfriend for a month.

Lleva un mes sin ver a su novia.
He hasn't seen his girlfriend for a month.

Hace tiempo que no trabajamos.
We haven't worked for some time.

Llevamos tiempo sin trabajar.
We haven't worked for some time.

Hace unos días que no me llaman.
They haven't called me in several days.

Llevan unos días sin llamarme.
They haven't called me in several days.

13.19 Write the equivalents, using one of the above patterns.

_____   _____
She hasn't called me for two weeks.   *I haven't seen him in ten years.*

_____   _____
They haven't worked here for a long time.   *We haven't eaten for three hours.*

13.20 Answer the following questions.

¿Hace cuánto tiempo que no ves a tu mejor amigo/a?

¿Cuánto tiempo llevas sin comer?

¿Hace cuánto tiempo que no te llama alguien?

13.21 Write a question for each of the following answers.

Hace mucho tiempo que no voy al cine.

Llevamos doce horas sin dormir.

Lleva cinco horas sin descansar.

What If I Want to Give the Actual Time That Something Began?

To ask when something began, ask:

¿Desde cuándo . . . ?
Since when . . . ?

Observe the following.

Trabajo aquí desde el 10 de agosto.
I've worked here since the 10th of August.

Ella es la directora desde 1988.
She's been the director since 1988.

Te estamos esperando desde las nueve de la mañana.
We've been waiting for you since 9:00 a.m.

Pedro enseña en la universidad desde 1996.
Pedro has been teaching at the university since 1996.

13.22 Write the pattern.

To tell the actual time that a current activity began, use _____ + the time. Use
el tiempo presente or a conjugated form of **estar** + _____ .

13.23 Write the equivalents.

_____

We've been here since 10 a.m.

_____

They've been watching TV since 4 o'clock.

_____

She's been going out with him since March.

_____

I've been studying for the exam since Monday.

Don't Forget

Use the verb in *el tiempo presente* or *estar en tiempo presente* followed by a *gerundio* even though English uses a different tense.

13.24 Practice answering the following questions in complete sentences; then listen to them on the recording, pausing it to answer them again. After you have given your answer, a speaker will give his own personal answer, which will probably not be exactly like yours. Other acceptable answers are given in the Answer Key in the Appendix.

 ¿Dónde vives?

¿Desde cuándo vives en ese lugar?

¿Dónde trabaja tu mejor amigo?

¿Desde cuándo trabaja en ese lugar?

In this chapter you have been using **el tiempo presente** to express activities that are going on at the present time. English expresses these quite differently, so it's a good idea to review these constructions with this in mind. Practice by asking yourself how long you've been doing certain things, and by asking your friends how long they've been living here and doing the things they've been doing. **Ahora, ¿estás cansado? ¿Cuánto tiempo llevas sin descansar?**

CHAPTER 14

Telling Intentions and Plans

Do I Need to Read This Chapter?

➡ Do I know how to ask someone for a favor—or offer to do one for somebody?

➡ Can I express a commitment to do something?

➡ Can I say in Spanish what my plans are, and ask others about theirs?

➡ Do I know how to express what people like to do, and what they want, hope, or prefer to do in the future?

➡ Do I know how to say what I am obligated to do, what I need to do, and ask others the same?

➡ Can I state my abilities—and ask others about theirs?

➡ Do I know how to ask "why?" and answer "because"?

Get Started

Read, listen to, and memorize the following dialogue.

Dialogue 26

Germán, ¿estás bien?
German, are you OK?

Realmente, no. Me siento muy mal.
¿Te quedas aquí conmigo un rato?
*Actually, no. I feel really bad. Will you stay
here with me a while?*

Claro que sí. ¿Qué te pasa?
Of course. What's the matter?

No sé. Estoy mareado. Además, me
duele mucho el estómago.
*I don't know. I'm dizzy—and my stomach
hurts.*

Tienes que hablar con el médico. Lo
llamo ahora mismo.
*You need to talk to the doctor. I'll call him right
now.*

Gracias. Su número está aquí en mi
agenda. Ay, sí, necesito alguna
medicina.
*Thanks. His number is here in my address
book. Oh, I do need some medicine.*

Germán, el médico dice que te puede
ver en una hora. Voy a buscar el
coche y te espero en frente de la casa
dentro de 30 minutos. Silvia se va a
quedar aquí contigo.
*German, the doctor says he can see you in an
hour. I'm going to get the car and I'll wait for
you out front in 30 minutes. Silvia's going to
stay here with you.*

Gracias, amigo. Oye, Silvia, ¿me
haces un favor?
*Thanks, pal. Listen, Silvia, will you do me
a favor?*

¿Qué puedo hacer?
What can I do?

Por favor, llama a mi jefe y dile que no
voy a poder trabajar hoy. Estoy muy
enfermo.
*Please call my boss and tell him I'm not going
to work today. I'm really sick.*

To Ask and Offer Favors in Spanish

To ask a favor:

¿Me ayudas?	¿Me haces un favor?	¿Me llevas a casa?
Will you help me?	*Will you do me a favor?*	*Will you take me home?*

¿Me compras un helado?	¿Me traes el periódico?
Will you buy me an ice cream?	*Will you bring me the newspaper?*

To offer a favor:

¿Te ayudo?	¿Te llevo a casa?	¿Te traigo algo?
Can I help you?	*Shall I take you home?*	*Can I bring you anything?*

◇ **Test Yourself**

14.1 Complete the following.

To ask and offer favors, use **el tiempo** _____ in the form of a

_____ .

14.2 Write the equivalents.

_____	_____	_____
Will you call me?	*Can I buy you anything?*	*Will you fix my car?*

_____	_____	_____
Shall I read it to you?	*Will you bring me a drink?*	*Shall I open the window for you?*

To Assure Someone That You Will Do Something

Look at these examples.

Te llamo mañana.	Lo hago esta tarde.
I'll call you tomorrow.	*I'll do it this afternoon.*

Nos vemos pronto.	Estoy aquí a las ocho.
We'll see each other soon.	*I'll be here at eight.*

Luego te cuento.	Nos hablamos esta noche.
I'll tell you later.	*We'll talk tonight.*

14.3 Complete the following.

To make a commitment or promise that you intend to do something, use **el tiempo** _____ .

14.4 Write the equivalents.

_____   _____   _____

I'll see you at six.   *We'll be here at eight o'clock.*   *I'll help you tomorrow.*

To Express Future Activities in Spanish

First, let's look at the words we need to indicate the future.

en seguida *right away*	mañana *tomorrow*	en julio *in July*
pronto *soon*	mañana por la mañana *tomorrow morning*	el próximo mes *next month*
luego *later*	pasado mañana *the day after tomorrow*	el próximo verano *next summer*
más tarde *later*	el lunes *on Monday*	el próximo año *next year*
después *later*	el fin de semana *on the weekend*	el año que viene *next year*
esta tarde *this afternoon*	la próxima semana *next week*	en cinco años *in five years*
esta noche *tonight*	la semana que viene *next week*	de ahora en adelante *from now on*

Look at the following sentences that tell about scheduled events and activities.

El tren sale a las ocho y diez.
The train leaves at 8:10.

Las clases empiezan pasado mañana.
Classes begin the day after tomorrow.

Salgo para España el 13 de julio.
I leave for Spain on the 13th of July.

Tengo una cita con el médico el viernes.
I have an appointment with the doctor on Friday.

Mañana estoy en Buenos Aires.
Tomorrow I'll be in Buenos Aires.

14.5 Complete the following.

Use **el tiempo** _____ to indicate scheduled activities.

14.6 Write the equivalents.

_____   _____

We leave at six.   *They go to Costa Rica next week.*

_____   _____

The plane leaves at nine.   *We'll be at the beach all summer.*

_____   _____

The bus arrives at 4 p.m.   *She has an appointment tomorrow morning.*

It's a Wrap Look in your **agenda** and write in Spanish the activities you have scheduled for next week. Tell when and where they will take place.

To Say Where You're Going and How You're Getting There

Observe the following sentences.

¿Adónde vas este verano?   Voy a Nueva York.
Where are you going this summer?   *I'm going to New York.*

¿Cómo vas?   Voy en tren.
How are you going?   *I'm going on the train.*

Here are other expressions you can use with **ir**.

a pie	en coche	en bicicleta	en bus	en avión	en barco
on foot	*in a car*	*on a bike*	*on the bus*	*by plane*	*by boat*

Observe the following verbs that indicate movement from one place to another.

caminar	manejar	viajar	volar (ue)	correr
walk	*drive*	*travel*	*fly*	*run*

Camino a mi casa.   Volamos a Europa.
I'm walking home.   *We're flying to Europe.*

¿Cuándo viajas a Costa Rica?   ¿Corren al parque esta tarde?
When are you traveling to Costa Rica? *Are you all running to the park this afternoon?*

Maneja a la oficina.   No van a ninguna parte esta tarde.
He's driving to the office.   *They're not going anywhere this afternoon.*

14.7 Complete the following.

Verbs that express movement from one place to another are followed by _____ , to indicate destination.

Answer the following questions.

¿Viajas el próximo verano? ¿Adónde? ¿Cómo?
¿Adónde vas mañana? ¿Cómo vas?

To Express Plans

Look at the following sequences that indicate what people plan to do or what they expect that others will do in the future.

¿Qué vas a hacer?   Voy a ver el video.
What are you going to do?   *I'm going to watch the video.*

¿Qué va a hacer Guillermo?   Va a hablar con su mamá.
What's Guillermo going to do?   *He's going to talk to his mother.*

¿Cuándo van a comer ustedes?   Vamos a comer a las ocho.
When are you all going to eat?   *We're going to eat at eight o'clock.*

¿A quién van a conocer ellos?   Van a conocer a mi jefe.
Who are they going to meet?   *They're going to meet my boss.*

14.8 Write the pattern.

To express what one expects will happen in the future, use a conjugated form of _____ + _____ + a verb in the _____ form.

14.9 Write the equivalents.

_____	_____	_____
I'm going to eat.	*Are you going to watch TV?*	*She's going to cook.*
_____	_____	_____
They're going to work.	*Are you all going to walk?*	*He's going to go out.*
_____	_____	_____
Are you all going to read?	*I'm not going to study.*	*She's going to rest.*

14.10 Practice answering the following questions in complete sentences; then listen to them on the recording, pausing it to answer them again. After you have given your answer, a speaker will give his own personal answer, which will probably not be exactly like yours. Other acceptable answers are given in the Answer Key in the Appendix.

¿Qué vas a hacer mañana?

¿Cuándo va a ir a tu casa tu mejor amigo?

¿Qué van a hacer tú y tus amigos la próxima semana?

¿Quién te va a llamar por teléfono?

¿A quién vas a llamar?

14.11 Make questions for the following answers.

Vamos a comer afuera.

Voy a ver la película "Amor perdido".

Van a salir mañana por la tarde.

Va a volver el próximo verano.

Quick Tip

Be careful not to use the *estar + -ndo* construction to express future activities. Compare the English and Spanish:

Voy a salir para España mañana.
I'm going to leave for Spain tomorrow. I'm leaving for Spain tomorrow.

Following is a common way to express the necessity of an action. Observe these sequences.

¿Qué tienes que hacer mañana?
What do you have to do?

Tengo que limpiar la casa.
I have to clean the house.

¿Qué tiene que hacer tu amigo?
What does your friend have to do?

Tiene que estudiar.
He has to study.

¿Qué tienen que hacer ustedes?
What do you all have to do?

Tenemos que practicar.
We have to practice.

¿Qué tienen que hacer ellos?
What do they have to do?

Tienen que ir a casa.
They have to go home.

14.12 Write the rule.

To express a personal need to do something, conjugate the verb _____ , add _____ , then add the _____ form of another verb.

14.13 Write the equivalents.

_____   _____   _____

We have to eat.   *You all have to rest.*   *She has to read the article.*

_____   _____   _____

He has to go home.   *I have to work.*   *You have to study.*

To Use Reflexive and Object Pronouns with These Patterns

Observe the following examples.

- With a reflexive pronoun:

  Voy a quedarme en casa.   Me voy a quedar en casa.
  I'm going to stay home.   *I'm going to stay home.*

  Tengo que irme ahora.   Me tengo que ir ahora.
  I have to go now.   *I have to go now.*

- With a direct object:

  Voy a llamarte mañana.   Te voy a llamar mañana.
  I'm going to call you tomorrow.   *I'm going to call you tomorrow.*

  Tengo que verte mañana.   Te tengo que ver mañana.
  I have to see you tomorrow.   *I have to see you tomorrow.*

- With an indirect object:

  Voy a decirte la verdad.   Te voy a decir la verdad.
  I'm going to tell you the truth.   *I'm going to tell you the truth.*

  Tengo que decirte la verdad.   Te tengo que decir la verdad.
  I have to tell you the truth.   *I have to tell you the truth.*

- With an indirect and a direct object:

  Voy a decírtela.   Te la voy a decir.
  I'm going to tell it to you.   *I'm going to tell it to you.*

  Tengo que decírtela.   Te la tengo que decir.
  I have to tell it to you.   *I have to tell it to you.*

- With an indirect object and a **verbo psicológico**:

  Va a molestarte.   Te va a molestar.
  It's going to bother you.   *It's going to bother you.*

  Van a gustarle.   Le van a gustar.
  They're going to please him.   *They're going to please him.*

14.14 Now write the patterns.

The reflexive, direct, and indirect objects can be placed either _____ the conjugated verb or attached to the _____ .

14.15 Write the equivalents, using one of the above patterns.

_____   _____
We have to sit down.   *I have to lie down.*

_____   _____
I'm going to call you.   *We're going to miss them* (a nuestros abuelos).

_____   _____
They're going to give it (el cuadro) *to you.*   *You have to show it* (la foto) *to her.*

_____   _____
It's going to enchant you.   *It's going to fascinate them.*

Expressing Desire, Possibility, and Need of Activity

Often the future is less structured—and we talk about the things we want to do, can or cannot do, need to do.

Observe the following examples.

Quiero bailar.   No queremos salir.
I want to dance.   *We don't want to go out.*

¿Quieres comer?   ¿Quieren ver la película?
Do you want to eat?   *Do you all want to watch the movie?*

Quiere descansar.   Quieren dormir.
She wants to rest.   *They want to sleep.*

14.16 Write the pattern.

To express "want to do something," use a conjugation of the verb _____ followed by the _____ of the verb that indicates the desired activity.

14.17 Express the following.

_____   _____
I want to sleep.   *He doesn't want to cook.*

_____   _____
She wants to work.   *They want to go home.*

_____   _____
I don't want to study.   *We want to have a party.*

_____   _____
What do you want to do?   *What do you all want to do tomorrow?*

14.18 Answer the following questions.

　　¿Qué quieres hacer mañana?

　　¿Adónde quieren ir tus amigos el próximo verano?

　　¿A qué hora quieren comer tú y tu amigo esta tarde?

　　¿Con quién quieres salir el fin de semana?

14.19 Make questions for the following answers.

　　Sí, quiero ir al cine contigo.

　　Queremos comer en un restaurante mexicano.

　　Quieren ir al museo mañana por la tarde.

　　Quiere hacer una fiesta en su casa el próximo viernes.

Here are some other verbs that indicate necessity, desire, obligation, and ability to perform activities.

-ar	-er	-ir
necesitar *need to*	deber *be obligated to*	preferir (ie i) *prefer to, would rather*
pensar (ie) *plan to*	poder (ue) *be able to*	
	saber *know how to*	

Look at the following examples.

Necesito encontrar trabajo.
I need to find work.

Pienso hacer una fiesta.
I'm planning to have a party.

Debo pagar mis impuestos.
I am obligated to pay my taxes.

No puedo ir a la fiesta.
I can't go to the party.

No sé tocar el violín. Sé tocar la guitarra.
I don't know how to play the violin. I know how to play the guitar.

Sé manejar, pero no puedo manejar porque no tengo coche.
I know how to drive, but I can't drive because I don't have a car.

Puedo ir al concierto, pero prefiero ir al cine.
I can go to the concert, but I would rather go to the movies.

14.20 Write the patterns.

To indicate the necessity of doing something, use a conjugated form of _____ + an _____ .

To indicate a plan to do something, use a conjugated form of _____ + an _____ .

To indicate a learned skill, use a conjugated form of _____ + an _____ .

To indicate a preference for doing something, use a conjugated form of _____ + an _____ .

To indicate the possibility of doing something, use a conjugated form of _____ + an _____ .

To indicate an obligation to do something, use a conjugated form of _____ + an _____ .

Quick Tip

As always, don't try to translate the English words. Instead, think of the function of each word in Spanish, and use it according to the Spanish pattern.

14.21 Now write the equivalents.

_____   _____
I need to study tonight.   *We are required to be in class at 8 a.m.*

_____	_____
They want to talk to us soon.	*She can't go tomorrow.*
_____	_____
He doesn't know how to swim.	*He can't swim today, because he's sick.*
_____	_____
I would rather dance.	*Do you know how to drive a car?*
_____	_____
You all can come with us next week.	*What do you plan to do on Sunday?*

14.22 Now answer these questions.

¿Qué deben hacer los estudiantes?

¿Dónde podemos comer bien en tu ciudad?

¿Qué piensa hacer tu mejor amigo mañana?

¿Qué prefieres hacer, trabajar o descansar?

14.23 Make a question for each of the following answers.

No, no puedo trabajar hoy.

Necesitamos comprar pan.

No sabe jugar fútbol.

Prefiero ver otra película.

Don't Forget

You can say how you feel about activities with the following expressions:
me gusta / me encanta / me fascina / me molesta followed by an infinitive.

To Say *Why?* and *Because*

All of these expressions are useful for answering the question **¿por qué?** Look at the following examples.

¿Por qué no vas al cine? No puedo ir porque no tengo dinero.
Why don't you go to the movies? *I can't go because I don't have any money.*

No quiero ir porque me molesta ese actor.
I don't want to go because that actor bothers me.

No puedo ir porque debo trabajar.
I can't go because I have to work.

No puedo ir porque tengo que estudiar.
I can't go because I have to study.

No voy a ir porque prefiero ir al concierto.
I'm not going because I would rather go to the concert.

¿Por qué no baila Víctor?   No baila porque no sabe bailar.
Why isn't Victor dancing?   *He's not dancing because he doesn't know how to dance.*

No debe bailar, porque está enfermo.
He's not supposed to dance because he's sick.

14.24 Write the rule.

To ask the question "why?" use _____ .

To say "because," use _____ .

14.25 Practice answering the following questions in complete sentences; then listen to them on the recording, pausing it to answer them again. After you have given your answer, a speaker will give his own personal answer, which will probably not be exactly like yours. Other acceptable answers are given in the Answer Key in the Appendix.

 ¿Por qué estudias español?

¿Qué te gusta hacer los fines de semana? ¿Por qué?

¿Qué no te gusta hacer? ¿Por qué?

¿Quieres viajar a un país de habla hispana? ¿Por qué?

14.26 Write questions for the following answers.

No voy a verla porque tengo que trabajar.

Sí, la quiero ver porque me fascina.

No puede ir a la fiesta porque está enfermo.

No van a la playa porque prefieren ir a las montañas.

Ahora sí sabes bastante español. Repasa todos los capítulos de este libro las veces necesarias para hablar con fluidez. Sigue hablando español con tus amigos, y recuerda que "querer es poder".

Epílogo

Do you remember the grammar test with the nonsense words at the beginning of this book? Here is a similar one in Spanish. Read the following sentence, whose content words are nonsense, then answer the questions. Check your answers in the Appendix.

La chila lace en el obinuo y se barta con su habo.

1. How many "actors" are there in this sentence?
2. Is the actor male or female?
3. What would one of the opposite sex be called?
4. What does **la chila** do first?
5. Where does **la chila** do this?
6. What else does **la chila** do?
7. Who or what is **la chila** with?
8. How could you say that **la chila** plans to do the same thing next week?
9. If you were doing this second activity, how could you state that?
10. How could you say that you can't do this activity tomorrow because you have to do something else?

¡Felicidades! ¡Ya sabes bastante español!

Appendix

Answer Key

1.1 At the beginning and end of an exclamation.   No.

1.2 At the beginning and end of a question.   No.

1.3 ¡Bienvenidos!   Buenas tardes, Buenas noches   ¡Cuidado!   Buenos días   Buen provecho   Con permiso   Gracias   Feliz cumpleaños   ¡Salud!   Perdón   ¡Socorro!   Buenas tardes   Por favor   De nada   Mucho gusto, Encantado/a   Hasta luego   Adiós   Que le vaya bien

3.1 mi   su   su   su   mi   su   su   su

3.2 ¿Quién?   ¿De dónde?   ¿Cuál es . . . ?

3.3 no   no

3.4 Soy _____ . Mi nombre es _____ .   Soy de _____ .   Es _____ .   Es de _____ .

3.5 ¿Cuál es su nombre?   ¿Quién es su amigo?   ¿De dónde es?   ¿De dónde es?   ¿Es usted de España?

3.6 el   la   -a   -a

3.7 -a   -a   -e   lowercase

3.8 la mexicana   el costarricense   la guatemalteca   el chileno   la señora   el estadounidense   el español   la niña   el hondureño

3.9 2   el   la

3.10 de la   del, del   del, de la

3.11 Mi nombre es _____ .   Soy de _____ .   Sí, soy (No, no soy) del norte.
Es _____ .   Es de _____ .   Es de _____ .

3.12 ¿Quién es el señor?   ¿De dónde es la Sra. Bravo?   ¿Cuál es su nombre?   ¿Es de la
capital?   ¿Es usted de Argentina?   ¿Es usted de Buenos Aires?

3.13 -es   -s   los   las

3.14 los nombres   el profesor   la mexicana   las uruguayas   el paraguayo   los barrios
la peruana   las ciudades   el lugar   las naciones   la vecindad   los estados   la
amiga   el vecino

3.15 mi   mis   su   sus   -s

3.16 mi   sus   su   sus   sus   mi   sus   su

3.17 ¿Quién . . . ?   ¿Quiénes . . . ?   ¿De qué país . . . ?   ¿De qué ciudad . . . ?   ¿De qué
parte . . . ?

3.18 Soy de _____ .   Sí, soy (No, no soy) del centro del país.   Es de _____ .
Sí, son (No, no son) de Chile.

3.19 ¿De dónde es él (ella)?   ¿Son ustedes de La Paz?   ¿Es de Uruguay?   ¿De qué
parte de Perú son?   ¿De qué ciudad es usted?

3.20 el abuelo   la abuela   el nieto   la nieta   el padre   la madre   el hijo   la hija   el
hermano   la hermana   el tío   la tía   el sobrino   la sobrina   el primo   la prima
el suegro   la suegra   el cuñado   la cuñada

3.21 el padre de José

3.22 feminine   masculine

3.23 Pedro y María son los padres de Ana.   José y Ana son los hijos de Pedro.   Elena es
la tía de Jorge. José es el tío de Jorge.   Juana es la prima de Luisa. Jorge es el primo
de Luisa.   Luisa es la nieta de María. Juana es la nieta de María.   Luisa y Susana
son las sobrinas de Ana.

3.24 Soy. . . _____ .

3.25 Es la esposa del Dr. Páez.   Es abogada.   Son médicos.   Es médico.   Es ginecólogo.
Los hijos de Ángeles y Carolina son estudiantes.   Su profesor es el Dr. Chávez.

3.26 el   la   -ora   la actriz   a male or female   -a   la modelo   la piloto   la médico

3.27 and   words that begin with the letter i or the letters hi.

3.28 sino   No, no soy profesor, sino estudiante.

3.29 Es la profesora de mi hijo.   Es profesora.   Es el abogado de mi vecino.   Es abogado.

3.30 Soy _____ .   Soy de _____ .   Soy _____ .   Su nombre
es _____ .   Es de _____ .   Es _____ .   Son _____
y _____ .   Sí, son (No, no son) mis primos.   Son del _____ .   Son
de _____ .

3.31 ¿Es usted Manolo?   ¿De qué parte del país es Sara?   ¿Son nicaragüenses?   ¿Cuál
es la profesión de José y Juan?   ¿Es Enrique el padre de _____ ?   ¿Es Marcos su hermano?

4.1 soltero   atlético   exitoso   culto   serio   responsable   divertido

4.2 soltera   atractiva   vivaz   no muy alta

4.3 agradable   simpático   alegre   egoísta   joven   hábil

4.4 arrogante   amigable   audaz   vivaz   exigente

4.5 -e   they end in -ista   they end in a consonant

4.6 -e   -ista   consonante   -s   -es

4.7 lo   before

4.8 Soy. . .   Es . . .   Son . . .   Sí, (No, no) es idealista. Sí, lo es. No, no lo es.

4.9 ¿Cómo es _____ ?   ¿Cómo son _____ y _____ ?   ¿Es usted pesimista?   ¿Es (*adjetivo*) usted?

4.10 -a   -dora   -a is deleted

4.11 habladora   pequeños   listas   bueno   after them

4.12 un   una   un   una

4.13 Soy estudiante.   Soy un(a) estudiante responsable.   Es ingeniero.   Es un ingeniero hábil.   Es contadora.   Es una contadora buena.   Son cocineros.   Son (unos) cocineros excelentes.   ¿Es programador(a)?   ¿Es especialista?

4.14 Es el hermano de Marta.   Es médico.   Es un médico muy famoso.

4.15 más baja que Elena   tan baja como Sonia   tan alta como Elena

4.16 mayor que   el/la mayor   menor que   el/la menor que

4.17 mejor que   el/la mejor de todos/as   peor que   el/la peor de todos/as

4.18 -e   -s   -n   -emos

4.19 La mamá tiene el pelo negro.   La mamá tiene el pelo largo.   El papá tiene la barba negra.   El papá tiene la barba larga.   La niña tiene los ojos negros.

4.20 Tiene los ojos bonitos.   Tengo el pelo largo.   Tenemos los ojos pardos.   Mi amigo tiene los pies pequeños.   Tiene los brazos musculosos.   Las muchachas tienen el pelo rizado.   Los hombres tienen los hombros grandes.

4.21 Soy _____ .   Tengo _____ años.   Tiene el pelo _____ . _____ y _____ tienen los ojos _____ .   Sí, (No, no) son responsables. Sí, lo son. No, no lo son.

4.22 ¿Tiene _____ el pelo negro?   ¿Es generoso _____ ?   ¿Cómo tienen los ojos Cristina y Daniel?   ¿Cómo son _____ y _____ ?

5.1 Who is it from?   Whose is it?

5.2 ¿Qué es esto?   Es un libro.   ¿De quién es?   Es de Juan.   ¿Qué es eso?   Es una tarjeta de crédito.   ¿De quién es?   Es de la Sra. Díaz.   ¿Qué son estos?   Son (unos) coches.   ¿De quiénes son?   Son de Ana y de Raúl.   ¿Qué son esos?   Son (unas) bicicletas.   ¿De quiénes son?   Son de Carlos y de Pedro.   ¿Qué es esto? ¿De quién es?   Es de Jimena.   ¿De quién es?   Es del novio de Jimena.

5.3 Es roja.   Es grande.   Son redondas.   Son blancos y medio grandes.

5.4 tú   usted, él, ella   ustedes, ellos, ellas   nosotros, nosotras

5.5 Tengo _____ .   Quiero _____ .   Tiene _____ .   Quiere _____ .   Sí (No, no) tenemos una computadora.   Sí, (No, no) queremos una computadora nueva.   Sí, (No, no) tenemos vecinos.   Sí, (No, no) tienen un coche.

5.6 ¿Tienes un coche grande?   ¿Tienes una casa bonita?   ¿Qué tiene tu amiga?   ¿Tienen un apartamento tus amigos?   ¿Qué tienen ustedes?   ¿Tienen ustedes zapatos nuevos?

5.7 lo   la   los   las   before

5.8 Sí, las quiero.   No, no lo quiero.   No, no la quiero.   No, no los quiero.

5.9 -dad   -ión   -ía   -za   -ud   -miento

5.10 la bondad   el fracaso   la salud   la fealdad   el amor   la pobreza   la sabiduría   la indiferencia   la tranquilidad, la paz

5.11 Sí, (No, no) lo quiero.   Sí, (No, no) lo tienen.   _____ la tiene.   Sí, (No, no) lo queremos.

5.12 ¿Tienes _____ ? ¿Quiere tu amigo _____ ? ¿Quieren ustedes _____ ? Tienen tus amigos _____ ? Tienen ustedes _____ ?

5.13 Es el maestro de español. Su nombre es Elena. Hay cinco. Hay treinta y dos.

5.14 ¿Cuántos . . . ? ¿Cuántas . . . ?

5.15 algo alguien nada nadie no

5.16 tres sesenta y cuatro setenta y dos treinta y uno quinientos cuarenta y seis siete mil ochocientos noventa y dos

6.1 Son las cinco. Son las seis. Son las siete. Son las ocho. Son las nueve. Son las diez. Son las once. Son las doce.

6.2 Son las tres y cuarto de la madrugada. Son las cuatro y media de la tarde. Son las siete y cinco de la mañana. Son las once menos veinte de la noche.

6.3 lunes, Monday lowercase después de antes de hoy

6.4 Es lunes. Es sábado. Es sábado. Hay siete. Es _____ .

6.5 ¿Qué día es? ¿Cuántos días hay en una semana? ¿Qué son sábado y domingo? ¿Qué día es antes del viernes (después del miércoles)? ¿Cuál es el primer día de la semana?

6.6 febrero abril noviembre enero doce

6.7 lowercase el primero

6.8 Es el veinte de junio. Es el seis de octubre. Es el treinta de mayo. Es el dieciocho de abril.

6.9 el primer el tercer la primera la tercera el primero la primera

6.10 el primer año la tercera casa la primera hora el tercer edificio la primera el tercero

6.11 El concierto es el lunes. Hoy es viernes. La fiesta es el sábado. Hoy es martes. La reunión es el miércoles. El ensayo es el domingo. Son las nueve de la noche. Es a las nueve de la mañana. Son las cuatro de la madrugada. Es a las cuatro de la tarde.

6.12 de por

6.13 ¿Qué hora es? Son las once de la mañana. ¿A qué hora es el concierto? Es a las nueve de la noche. ¿Cuándo es la fiesta? Es el sábado por la noche. ¿Dónde es la película? Es en el cine Rialto.

6.14 Tengo _____ Es el _____ Es el _____
Es por la _____ Es a la/las _____ Es en _____

6.15 a las seis de la mañana a las nueve y media de la mañana a la una y cuarto de la tarde a las nueve de la noche a las diez y media de la noche

7.1 estoy estamos estás están está está están estás, está, están

7.2 Estoy bien. ¿Estás bien? Estamos mejor. Están peor. Mi tío está más o menos. Los muchachos están mal.

7.3 Está _____ . Están _____ . Está _____ . Estoy _____ .

7.4 ¿Cómo están (ustedes)? ¿Cómo está _____ ? ¿Cómo están _____ y _____ ? ¿Cómo estás?

7.5 ¿Cómo estás? ¿Tienen prisa? ¿Cómo está tu amiga? ¿Qué tiene el muchacho? ¿Tienen miedo los niños?

7.6 Está _____ . Sí, (No, no) está limpio. Sí, (No, no) están sucios.

7.7 está rica   está fría   está lista

7.8 Soy responsable.   Soy sincero/a.   Estoy enfermo/a.   Estoy cansado/a.   Estás guapo/a.

7.9 es fascinante, están fascinadas   está intrigado, es interesante   son sorprendentes, estamos sorprendidos   están aburridos, es aburrido

8.1 ¿Dónde está Cuba? Está en el Caribe. Está al sur de Florida.   ¿Dónde están Uruguay y Paraguay? Están en América del Sur.   ¿Dónde está Nicaragua? Está en América Central, en la costa del Caribe.

8.2 Soy de _____ .   Está en _____ .   Está al sur (norte, este, oeste) de _____ .   Está en el centro (norte, sur, este, oeste) del municipio.

8.3 Estoy aquí.   Estoy adentro.   La mesa está ahí.   La lámpara está cerca.   Hay una silla a la derecha.   El televisor está a la izquierda.   Mi cuarto está arriba.   Mi cocina está abajo.   Mi coche está afuera.   La casa de mi amigo está allí.

8.4 El banco está enfrente de la zapatería.   La biblioteca está al lado de la librería. Detrás de la escuela hay un parque.   El aeropuerto está lejos del bosque.   Hay un parque debajo de la oficina de correos.   La estación de trenes está cerca de la playa. Hay un supermercado entre el zoológico y el hospital.   La panadería está dentro del centro comercial.

8.5 conmigo   contigo

8.6 con él   con ellos/as   con ella   con nosotros/as   con ustedes

8.7 Es de _____ .   Está en _____ .   Estoy en _____ .   Estoy con _____ . / Estoy solo/a.   Tengo un(a) _____ .   Es a la/las _____ .   Es en _____ .   Está en _____ .   Sí, (No, no) está cerca de mi casa.

8.8 ¿Está tu amigo contigo?   ¿Dónde está _____ ?   ¿Dónde están _____ y _____ ?   ¿Dónde está los Estados Unidos?   ¿Dónde es la película?   ¿De dónde son ustedes?

9.1 Hace mucho frío.   Hace mucho calor.   Hace buen tiempo.   Hace un poco de frío. Hace frío.   Hace fresco.

9.2 Hace buen tiempo en la primavera y en el otoño.   Hace calor en el verano.   Hace frío en el invierno.   Llueve mucho.   No nieva nunca.   Hace buen tiempo todo el año.

10.1 soy, estoy, tengo, quiero   eres, estás, tienes, quieres   es, está, tiene, quiere   somos, estamos, tenemos, queremos   son, están, tienen, quieren

10.2 -ar   -er   -ir

10.3 -o   -amos

10.4 -a   -an

10.5 -a   -as   -an

10.6 bailo, cantamos, cocinas, compran   contesta, escucha, limpiamos, pregunto   usas, trabajo, lava, habla   manejan, pasamos tiempo, estudias, practico

10.7 ¿Hablas español?   ¿Trabaja María?   ¿Manejan Ana y su hermana?   ¿Cocinan ustedes?   ¿Hablamos mucho?   ¿Baila Enrique?

10.8 Sí, estudio español.   Sí, (No, no) hablamos mucho.   Sí, (No, no) trabaja.   Sí, (No, no) cantan.

10.9 ¿Lavan los coches?   ¿Escucha la música *rock* _____ ?   ¿Usas la computadora en casa?   ¿Contesta _____ el teléfono?

10.10 feminine   -mente

10.11 Ana María espera nerviosamente.   Horacio habla vulgarmente.   Manejan despaciosamente   Trajaba independientemente   Carlos contesta amablemente   Trabajo alegremente.

10.12 -ie   -ue   nosotros

10.13 comienzo, recuerdo   comienzas, recuerdas   comienza, recuerda   comienzan, recuerdan   comenzamos, recordamos

10.14 Las clases empiezan a las _____ .   Jugamos _____ .   Almuerza con _____ .   Sí, (No, no) recuerdo su nombre.

10.15 ¿Qué juega _____ ?   ¿A qué hora almuerzan?   ¿A qué hora comienza _____ ?   ¿Recuerdas?

10.16 -er   -o   -emos   -es   -en   -e   -en

10.17 respondemos   no comprende   venden   creo   ¿Corres?   bebe

10.18 Leo el periódico por la mañana (tarde, noche).   Sí, (No, no) corre.
Comemos _____ .   Venden pescado en el mercado.

10.19 ¿A qué hora comen _____ y _____ ?   ¿Comprendes?
¿Cuándo corres?   ¿Dónde venden el periódico?

10.20 -ie   -ue   last   nosotros   Yes.   -ie

10.21 entiendo   vuelve   quieren   perdemos   resuelve   leo   vende   queremos   ¿Entiendes? (¿Comprendes?)   creen   responde (contesta)   vuelvo

10.22 yo

10.23 traemos   saben   hago   ve   pongo   conoce   no sé   vemos   ¿Sabes?   conozco   ¿traes?   veo

10.24 Parece simpática.   Merecemos dinero.   No conozco a Mónica.   Obedecen.   No obedezco.   Parece aburrido.

10.25 Pierdo mi(s) _____ .   Conozco a _____ personas.
Leemos _____ .   Comen tacos y frijoles.   Sí, (No, no) sabe dónde estoy.

10.26 ¿Sabe la fecha de tu cumpleaños?   ¿A quién conoces aquí?   ¿A qué hora vuelven a la oficina?   ¿Dónde (Con quién) come?   ¿Conoces Bolivia?

10.27 recibo   abro   vivo   prefiero   recibes   abres   vives   prefieres   recibe   abre   vive   prefiere   recibimos   abrimos   vivimos   preferimos   reciben   abren   viven   prefieren

10.28 -ir   -o   -emos   -es   -e   -en   -e   -en   last   nosotros

10.29 duerme   asistimos   sirve   no miento   no mueren   dormimos   ¿Sirves?   asiste   servimos

10.30 Sí, (No, no) recibo muchas cartas.   Escriben email todos los días.   Vivo en _____ .   Duermo _____ horas.   Yo sirvo _____ sirve la comida en mi casa.   Vive con _____ .   Sí, (No, no) asisto a una clase de español.   Sí, (No, no) abro todo el email que recibo.   Sí, (No, no) es verdad.   Prefiero _____ .

10.31 ¿Duerme bien el niño?   ¿Qué helado prefieren?   ¿Muere el abuelo?   ¿Miente el novio?   ¿A qué hora sirven la cena?   ¿A qué colegio asiste ella?   ¿Dónde (Con quién) vive tu hermana?

10.32 yo

10.33 Salgo con _____ .   Salgo de mi casa a las _____ .   Salgo para _____ .

10.34 yo

10.35 que

10.36 Digo que es _____ . Dice que es muy bueno.

10.37 -y nosotros

10.38 Huimos ¿Construyes casas? Destruyen el edificio. No huyo. Construimos puentes. No destruye nada.

10.39 hear yo oigo

10.40 Oigo _____ . (No oiga nada.) Sí, (No, no) oye bien. _____ oye. (_____ y _____ oyen.) (No oye nadie.)

10.41 Soy (inteligente). Estoy (aquí).

10.42 a ¿adónde? a ninguna parte

10.43 Voy a _____ . Va a _____ . Sí, (No, no) vamos a la playa con mucha frecuencia. Vienen a mi casa _____ . Voy _____ .

10.44 ¿Adónde vas? ¿Cuándo van a _____ ? ¿Va contigo? ¿Adónde van?

11.1 me te se nos

11.2 Me despierto. Te vistes. Se lava los dientes. Se queja. Nos sentimos. Nos sentamos. Se quedan. Se afeita. Se maquilla. No se peinan. Me lavo la cara. Se lava las manos. Me baño. Se quita los zapatos. Nos reímos. Se divierten. Se vuelve loca. ¿Te aburres? Se cansan. Se levanta. Se pone el sombrero. Me enojo. Se enamoran. Se desespera.

11.3 ¿A qué hora se despierta? ¿Se quejan ustedes? ¿Se enojan ellos? ¿Cómo te sientes?

11.4 ¿Cuál es su nombre? Su nombre es José. ¿Cómo se llama? Se llama José. ¿Cuál es su nombre? Su nombre es Juanita. ¿Cómo se llama? Se llama Juanita. ¿Cuáles son los nombres de tus amigos? Sus nombres son Miguel y Juan. ¿Cómo se llaman tus amigos? Se llaman Miguel y Juan.

11.5 Me llamo _____ . Se llama _____ . Se llaman _____ y _____ . Se llama _____ .

11.6 Me ayudo. Se sirve. Nos hablamos. Se llaman. ¿Te cuidas? ¿Se ayudan?

11.7 Sí, (No, no) nos hablamos. Nos reunimos _____ . Me miro en el espejo todos los días. Todos nos servimos. Me levanto a las _____ . Se acuestan a las _____ .

11.8 a want love, care about

11.9 Quiero un coche. Quiero a mi amigo. Visitamos la escuela. Visitamos a los maestros. Mira el edificio. Mira a los estudiantes. Escucha la radio. No escucha a su madre. ¿Llamas a tu novio?

11.10 him, it her, it them them before

11.11 No lo queremos. Los escucho. María la ve. Lo quiere mucho. Lo quiere. La extraña.

11.12 me te lo la los las nos

11.13 Me ayuda. Me recoge. Me llaman. Te escogen. Te quiere. Te ayudamos. Los escucho. Los quiero. Los visita. Te quiero. ¿Me quieres? Te extraño. Nos extrañan. Nos llama. ¿Nos escuchas?

11.14 ¿A quién llamas? ¿Quién te llama? Llamo a mi papá. Mi papá me llama. ¿A quién visitan? ¿Quién los visita? Visitan a su abuela. Su abuela los visita.

11.15 _____ me llama. Llamo a _____ . _____ lo visita. Visita a _____ . _____ me quiere. Quiero a _____ .

11.16 ¿Extrañas a _____ y _____ ? ¿Con qué frecuencia llamas a tu mejor amigo _____ ? ¿Estudias español? ¿Estudian español? ¿Me quieres?

12.1 -ar   yo   doy

12.2 a nosotros, nos   a ti, te   a ustedes, les   a usted, le   a él, le   a ellos, les   a Juan, le   a Juan y Carlos, les   a ella, le   a ellas, les   a mi madre, le   a mi mamá y a mi hermana, les

12.3 subject   indirect object pronoun   verb/subject   direct object   a + name   A Ana le damos los libros Elena y yo.   A Ana le damos los libros.   Le damos los libros.

12.4 indirect object pronoun   subject   a + noun or pronoun

12.5 indirect object pronoun

12.6 Le doy los libros a él. Le doy los libros.   Maria te da las revistas a ti. Te de las revistas.   Te damos el coche a ti. Te damos el coche.   Sus primos le dan trabajo a él. Le dan trabajo.   ¿Le das dinero a ella? ¿Le das dinero?   ¿Tus amigos te dan dulces a ti? ¿Te dan dulces?   El jefe les da una oportunidad a ellos. Les da una oportunidad. El jefe no nos da nada a nosotros.   No nos da nada.

12.7 Le doy dinero a _____ . _____ me da dinero. Sí, le doy _____ . (No, no le doy nada.)   Sí, me da _____ . (No, no me da nada.)

12.8 Me muestra las fotos.   Le manda cartas.   Les devolvemos los regalos.   Le digo mis secretos.   Nos escriben cartas.   Le prepara la cena.   Me manda email.   Le compran flores.   Me explica las matemáticas.

12.9 _____ me dice sus secretos.   Le digo mis ideas más fantásticas a _____ . _____ y _____ me escriben email.   Les escribo email a _____ y a _____ .

12.10 ¿A quiénes les mandas tarjetas?   ¿Quiénes te muestran sus fotos?   ¿Quién te prepara la cena?   ¿A quién le escribes cartas de amor?   ¿Quién te presta dinero?

12.11 preguntar   indirect object pronoun   si

12.12 pedir   indirect object pronoun

12.13 Le pido los libros a Juan.   Le pregunto a Juan si los lee.   Le preguntamos a Juanita adónde va.   Nos responde que va a casa.   La profesora nos pide la tarea.   La profesora nos pregunta dónde está Juan.

12.14 Le pregunto _____ .   Me contesta que _____ .   Les pido _____ . Me dan _____ .

12.15 before   indirect object pronoun   direct object pronoun

12.16 Le pido el coche a mi padre.   Mi padre me lo da.   Le pedimos la receta a nuestra hermana.   Nos la da.   Me pides los libros.   Te los doy.   Le pido las llaves a mi hermano.   Me las da.

12.17 se

12.18 La profesora nos pide la tarea.   Se la damos.   Mi amigo me pide un periódico.   Se lo doy.   Ana y Berta le piden el coche a Juan.   Se lo da.   Le piden las llaves.   Se las da.

12.19 Sí, me dice sus ideas.   Me las dice _____ .   Sí, le digo mis secretos.   Se los digo _____ .

12.20 ¿Le das el _____ ?   ¿Les dice el _____ ?   ¿Te presta la _____ ? ¿Le manda el _____ ?

12.21 Me gusta el vestido. Me gusta. Me gusta la casa. Me gusta.

12.22 Me gustan los libros. Me gustan. Me gustan los coches. Me gustan.

12.23 Me encantan los zapatos. Me encantan estos zapatos. Me gusta la comida mexicana. Me gusta la comida aquí.

12.24 Le fascinan las clases. Le encantan los zapatos. Me interesan las novelas. Nos gustan los tacos. Me molesta el tráfico. Les fascina la película. ¿Te importan las notas? Nos aburre la clase. ¿Te gusta la música *rock*?

12.25 _____ me cae bien. _____ me cae mal. Me gusta _____ .
Le gusto a _____ . Quiero a _____ y a _____ . _____
y _____ me quieren. Sí, amo a _____ . (No, no amo a nadie.)
Sí, _____ me ama. (No, nadie me ama.)

12.26 ¿Te cae bien _____ ? ¿Cómo te cae (Qué te parece) _____ ? ¿Le gusta Gustavo? ¿Te molesta _____ ?

12.27 infinitive

12.28 Le aburre estudiar. Me encanta jugar fútbol. Me gusta ver fútbol. Le gusta caminar. Les fascina ir a fiestas. Le gusta dormir.

Me gusta _____ r. Me encanta _____ r. Me molesta _____ r.
Me fascina _____ r.

13.1 estar   -ndo

13.2 -ar, -er, -ir   -ando   -iendo

13.3 Está hablando. Estamos escribiendo. Están aprendiendo. ¿Estás escuchando? Está corriendo. Estoy preparando. Está cocinando. Estamos descubriendo. ¿Están comiendo?

13.4 -yendo   -iendo

13.5 -ir   gerund

13.6 Está sirviendo la comida. Están mintiendo. Está durmiendo. ¿Qué estás diciendo? No te estoy pidiendo dinero. No está muriendo.

13.7 Estoy haciendo este ejercicio. Está _____ . (No sé qué está haciendo.) No, no estoy aprendiendo francés, sino español. Sí, estoy _____ ndo . . . Sí, (No, no) estamos trabajando.

13.8 ¿Qué están haciendo? (¿Qué hacen?) ¿Con quién está trabajando _____ ? (¿Con quién trabaja?) ¿Qué están haciendo _____ y _____ ? (¿Qué hacen?) ¿Qué estás haciendo? (¿Qué haces?)

13.9 before   gerund

13.10 Me estoy vistiendo. (Estoy vistiéndome.) Nos estamos perdiendo. (Estamos perdiéndonos.) ¿Te estás durmiendo? (¿Estás durmiéndote?) ¿Se están cansando? (¿Están cansándose?) Se está despertando. (Está despertándose.) Se están enamorando. (Están enamorándose.)

13.11 Lo estoy comprando. (Estoy comprándolo.) Los estamos visitando. (Estamos visitándolos.) ¿Lo estás viendo? ¿Estás viéndolo? ¿Lo están vendiendo? (¿Están vendiéndolo?) Las está llamando. (Está llamándolas.) Nos están mirando. (Están mirándonos.)

13.12 Se la estoy mandando. (Estoy mandándosela.) Se las estamos mostrando. (Estamos mostrándoselas.) ¿Me lo estás comprando? (¿Estás comprándomelo?) Se lo están enseñando? (¿Están enseñándoselo?) Me los está vendiendo. (Está vendiéndomelos.) Nos la están explicando. (Están explicándonosla.)

13.13 hace   que

13.14 Hace cinco años que vivo aquí.   Hace diez años que trabaja aquí.   Hace varios meses que estudiamos español.   Hace seis semanas que están en México.

13.15 hace   que   gerund

13.16 Hace _____ que estoy viviendo aquí.   Hace _____ que estoy estudiando español.   Hace _____ que estoy haciendo estos ejercicios.

13.17 llevar   gerund

13.18 Llevo cuatro años estudiando.   Lleva tres meses buscando trabajo.   Llevamos dos horas viendo la televisión.   Llevan una hora jugando tenis.

13.19 Hace dos semanas que no me llama. (Lleva dos semanas sin llamarme.)   Hace diez años que no lo veo. (Llevo diez años sin verlo.)   Hace mucho tiempo que no trabajan aquí. (Llevan mucho tiempo sin trabajar aquí.)   Hace tres horas que no comemos. (Llevamos tres horas sin comer.)

13.20 Hace _____ que no lo (la) veo.   Llevo _____ sin comer.
Hace _____ que no me llama _____ .

13.21 ¿Hace cuánto tiempo que no vas al cine?   ¿Cuánto tiempo llevan sin dormir?
¿Cuánto tiempo llevas sin descansar?

13.22 desde   gerund

13.23 Estamos aquí desde las diez de la mañana.   Están viendo (Ven) la tele desde las cuatro.   Está saliendo (Sale) con él desde marzo.   Estoy estudiando (Estudio) desde el lunes.

13.24 Vivo en _____ .   Estoy viviendo (Vivo) ahí desde _____ .   Trabaja en _____ .   Está trabajando (Trabaja) ahí desde _____ .

14.1 presente   question

14.2 ¿Me llamas?   ¿Te compro algo?   ¿Me arreglas el coche?   ¿Te lo leo?   ¿Me traes un refresco?   ¿Te abro la ventana?

14.3 presente

14.4 Te veo a las seis.   Estamos aquí a las ocho.   Te ayudo mañana.

14.5 presente

14.6 Salimos a las seis.   Van a Costa Rica la próxima semana.   El avión sale a las nueve.   Estamos en la playa todo el verano.   El autobús llega a las cuatro de la tarde.   Tiene una cita mañana por la mañana.

14.7 a   Sí, viajo a _____ en _____ .   No, no viajo el próximo verano.
Mañana voy a _____ en _____ .

14.8 ir   a   infinitive

14.9 Voy a comer.   ¿Vas a ver la televisión?   Va a cocinar.   Van a trabajar.   ¿Van a caminar?   Va a salir.   ¿Van a leer?   No voy a estudiar.   Va a descansar.

14.10 Voy a _____ .   Va a venir a mi casa _____ .   Vamos a _____ .
_____ me va a llamar. (No sé quién me va a llamar.)   Voy a llamar a _____ . (No voy a llamar a nadie.)

14.11 ¿Dónde van a comer?   ¿Qué película vas a ver?   ¿Cuándo van a salir?   ¿Cuándo va a volver?

14.12 tener   que   infinitive

14.13 Tenemos que comer.   Tienen que descansar.   Tiene que leer el artículo.   Tiene que ir a casa.   Tengo que trabajar.   Tienes que estudiar.

14.14 before   infinitive

14.15 Nos tenemos que sentar. (Tenemos que sentarnos.)   Me tengo que acostar. (Tengo que acostarme.)   Te voy a llamar. (Voy a llamarte.)   Los vamos a extrañar. (Vamos a extrañarlos.)   Te lo van a dar. (Van a dártelo.)   Se la tienes que mostrar. (Tienes que mostrársela.)   Te va a encantar. (Va a encantarte)   Les va a fascinar. (Va a fascinarles.)

14.16 querer   infinitive

14.17 Quiero dormir.   No quiere cocinar.   Quiere trabajar.   Quieren ir a casa.   No quiero estudiar.   Queremos hacer una fiesta.   ¿Qué quieres hacer?   ¿Qué quieren hacer mañana?

14.18 Quiero _____ .   Quieren ir a _____ .   Queremos comer a las _____ .   Quiero salir con _____ .

14.19 ¿Quieres ir al cine conmigo?   ¿Dónde quieren comer?   ¿Adónde quieren ir mañana? (¿Cuándo quieren ir al museo?)   ¿Qué quiere hacer? (¿Cuándo quiere hacer una fiesta en su casa?)

14.20 necesitar, infinitive   pensar, infinitive   saber, infinitive   preferir, infinitive   poder, infinitive   deber, infinitive

14.21 Necesito estudiar esta noche.   Debemos estar en clase a las ocho de la mañana. Quieren hablar con nosotros pronto.   No puede ir mañana.   No sabe nadar.   No puede nadar hoy porque está enfermo.   Prefiero bailar.   ¿Sabes manejar un coche? Pueden ir con nosotros la próxima semana.   ¿Qué piensas hacer el domingo?

14.22 Deben estudiar.   Pueden comer bien en el restaurante _____ . Piensa _____ .   Prefiero _____ .

14.23 ¿Puedes trabajar hoy?   ¿Qué necesitan comprar?   ¿Sabe jugar fútbol?   ¿Quieres ver esta película? (¿Qué película prefieres ver?)

14.24 ¿por qué?   porque

14.25 Lo estudio porque quiero aprenderlo (porque me gusta, porque . . .)   Me gusta _____ porque _____ .   No me gusta _____ porque _____ .   Sí, (No, no) quiero viajar a _____ porque _____ .

14.26 ¿Por qué no vas a ver la película?   ¿Quieres verla?   ¿Por qué no va a la fiesta? ¿Por qué no van a la playa?

Epílogo: 1. one   2. female   3. el chilo   4. lace   5. en el obinuo   6. se barta   7. su habo   8. Va a lacer (lacir) en el obinuo y va a bartarse con su habo.   9. Me estoy bartando. (Estoy bartándome.)   10. No puedo bartarme mañana porque tengo que _____ . (No me puedo bartar mañana porque tengo que _____ .)

Vosotros

Vosotros (**vosotras**) is the subject pronoun that in Spain represents the plural of **tú**—or "you all" to a group of friends. Following are the **vosotros** patterns for the uses covered in this book.

Chapters 1–9

ser: sois
¿Quiénes sois?   ¿De dónde sois?   ¿Cómo sois?
Who are you all?   *Where are you all from?*   *What are you all like?*

estar: estáis
¿Cómo estáis?   ¿Dónde estáis?   ¿Qué estáis haciendo?
How are you all?   *Where are you all?*   *What are you all doing?*

tener: tenéis
¿Qué tenéis?   ¿Tenéis hambre?   ¿Cuántos años tenéis?
What do you all have?   *Are you all hungry?*   *How old are you all?*

querer: queréis
¿Qué queréis?   ¿Queréis comer con nosotros?   Os quiero mucho.
What do you all want?   *Do you all want to eat with us?*   *I love you all.*

Chapter 10

-ar Verbs		*-er* Verbs		*-ir* Verbs	
trabajar:	trabajáis	comer:	coméis	vivir:	vivís
hablar:	habláis	aprender:	aprendéis	escribir:	escribís
escuchar:	escucháis	leer:	leéis	salir:	salís
		ver:	véis		

Stem-changing verbs		*Stem-changing verbs*		*Stem-changing verbs*	
empezar (ie):	empezáis	entender (ie):	entendéis	servir (i, i):	servís
pensar (ie):	pensáis	perder (ie):	perdéis	mentir (ie, i):	mentís
jugar (ue):	jugáis	volver (ue):	volvéis	dormir (ue, u):	dormís
almorzar (ue):	almorzáis	resolver (ue):	resolvéis	decir (i, i):	decís
				contribuir:	contribuís
				oír:	oís
				ir:	váis

¿Adónde váis?
Where are you all going?

Chapter 11: Verbs with Reflexive Pronouns

-ar Verbs		*-er* Verbs		*-ir* Verbs	
levantarse:	os levantáis	ponerse:	os ponéis	aburrirse:	os aburrís
cansarse:	os cansáis			reunirse:	os reunís
quejarse:	os quejáis				

Stem-changing verbs		*Stem-changing verbs*		*Stem-changing verbs*	
acostarse (ue):	os acostáis	volverse (ue):	os volvéis	dormirse (ue, u):	os dormís
sentarse (ie):	os sentáis	perderse (ie):	os perdéis	sentirse (i, i):	os sentís
				vestirse (i, i):	os vestís
				divertirse (ie, i):	os divertís
				irse:	os váis

¿Os váis?
Are you all leaving?

Chapter 12

dar: dáis

comprar: compráis

mandar: mandáis

Juan os da el dinero a vosotros.
Juan gives the money to you all.

Os lo da.
He gives it to you all.

¿Os gusta el chocolate?
Does chocolate appeal to you all?

¿Os molestan los niños?
Do the children bother you all?

Chapter 13

estar + pintar: estáis pintando

estar + vestirse: os estáis vistiendo
you are all getting dressed

¿Hace cuánto tiempo que vivís aquí?
How long have you been living here?

¿Cuánto tiempo lleváis viviendo aquí?
How long have you been living here?

Chapter 14

¿Me ayudáis? *Will you all help me?*	¿Qué tenéis que hacer? *What do you all have to do?*
¿Me hacéis un favor? *Will you all do me a favor?*	¿Queréis comer? *Do you all want to eat?*
¿Nos lleváis a casa? *Will you all take us home?*	¿Qué preferís hacer? *What would you all rather do?*
¿Adónde viajáis? *Where are you all traveling to?*	¿Podéis ir con nosotros? *Can you all go with us?*
¿Qué vais a hacer? *What are you all going to do?*	¿Qué os interesa hacer? *What are you all interested in doing?*

The possessive pronoun is **vuestro/a/os/as.**

Write the patterns.

To make the **vosotros** form in **el tiempo presente,** first remove the _____ , _____ , or _____ ending of the infinitive.

To **-ar** verbs, add _____ , placing a **tilde** over the _____ .*

To **-er** verbs, add _____ , placing a **tilde** over the _____ .*

To **-ir** verbs, add _____ , placing a **tilde** over the _____ .*

Verbs that have stem-changing indications (**ie, ue, i**) do _____ change in the **vosotros** form.

_____ is the reflexive, direct object, and indirect object pronoun that refers to **vosotros**.

Answers

-ar   -er   -ir   áis   -a   éis   -e   ís   -i   not   os

*sois (ir), dais (dar), veis (ver), and vais (ir) do not have a **tilde.**

Vocabulario personal

It is a good idea to keep a personal notebook to help you remember new words. Following is a format for organizing your words that will help you use them in the patterns you have been practicing in this book.

First, make four major sections. Reserve the first third of the notebook for nouns and the second third for verbs. Divide the remaining third into two sections—one for adjectives and one for adverbs.

Reserve several pages for each of the subcategories listed below, and divide each page as indicated. Add new words as you come across them, and practice using them according to the appropriate patterns.

Nouns

People
Masculino   **Femenino**

Nationalities
Masculino   **Femenino**

Jobs and professions
Masculino   **Femenino**

Places
Masculino   **Femenino**

Objects
Masculino   **Femenino**

Materials things are made of
Masculino   **Femenino**

Abstract aspects of life
Masculino   **Femenino**

Complaints and diseases
Masculino   **Femenino**

Events
Masculino   **Femenino**

Verbs

List verbs in their infinitive forms; indicate spelling changes in parentheses

Verbs that indicate movement from one place to another (**de . . . a**)

-ar   **-er**   **-ir**

Verbs that require reflexive pronouns

-ar   **-er**   **-ir**

Verbs that have direct objects but not indirect ones

-ar   **-er**   **-ir**

Verbs that indicate an exchange (require both a direct and an indirect object)

-ar   **-er**   **-ir**

Verbs that indicate the cause of a feeling (require an indirect object; have no direct object)

-ar   **-er**   **-ir**

Verbs that have no objects

-ar   **-er**   **-ir**

Adjectives

Personal characteristics

Descriptions of objects

Descriptions of events

Present conditions of people

Present conditions of things

Adverbs

Ways of doing things

Index

About the Author

Jean Yates currently teaches Spanish at George Washington University in Washington, D.C. She has taught both Spanish and English as a Second Language to high school, community college, and university students, as well as to adults at the workplace. She has a B.A. in Spanish, an M.A. in Linguistics, and a Ph.D. in Linguistics. She is a successful author of Spanish language–learning grammars and materials for Spanish-speaking learners of English.